UNDERSTANDING
BOBBIE ANN MASON

Understanding Contemporary American Literature
Matthew J. Bruccoli, Series Editor

Volumes on

Edward Albee • Nicholson Baker • John Barth • Donald Barthelme
The Beats • The Black Mountain Poets • Robert Bly
Raymond Carver • Chicano Literature
Contemporary American Drama
Contemporary American Horror Fiction
Contemporary American Literary Theory
Contemporary American Science Fiction
James Dickey • E. L. Doctorow • John Gardner • George Garrett
John Hawkes • Joseph Heller • Lillian Hellman • John Irving
Randall Jarrell • William Kennedy • Jack Kerouac
Ursula K. Le Guin • Denise Levertov • Bernard Malamud
Bobbie Ann Mason • Jill McCorkle • Carson McCullers
W. S. Merwin • Arthur Miller • Toni Morrison
Vladimir Nabokov • Gloria Naylor • Joyce Carol Oates
Tim O'Brien • Flannery O'Connor • Cynthia Ozick • Walker Percy
Katherine Anne Porter • Reynolds Price • Thomas Pynchon
Theodore Roethke • Philip Roth • Hubert Selby, Jr.
Mary Lee Settle • Isaac Bashevis Singer • Jane Smiley
Gary Snyder • William Stafford • Anne Tyler • Kurt Vonnegut
James Welch • Eudora Welty • Tennessee Williams • August Wilson

UNDERSTANDING
BOBBIE ANN MASON

Joanna Price

University of South Carolina Press

© 2000 University of South Carolina

Published in Columbia, South Carolina, by the
University of South Carolina Press

Manufactured in the United States of America

04   03   02   01   00   5   4   3   2   1

Library of Congress Cataloging-in-Publication Data

Price, Joanna, 1961–
    Understanding Bobbie Ann Mason / Joanna Price.
      p.   cm. — (Understanding contemporary American literature)
    Includes bibliographical references and index.
    ISBN 1-57003-381-1 (alk. paper)
    1. Mason, Bobbie Ann—Criticism and interpretation.
  2. Women and literature—United States—History—20th century.
  3. Rural conditions in literature.   4. Working class in literature.
  5. Country life in literature.   6. Kentucky—In literature.   I. Title.
II. Series.
PS3563.A7877 Z82   2000
813'.54—dc21   00-011152

For my parents

CONTENTS

EDITOR'S PREFACE

The volumes of *Understanding Contemporary American Literature* have been planned as guides or companions for students as well as good nonacademic readers. The editor and publisher perceive a need for these volumes because much of the influential contemporary literature makes special demands. Uninitiated readers encounter difficulty in approaching works that depart from the traditional forms and techniques of prose and poetry. Literature relies on conventions, but the conventions keep evolving; new writers form their own conventions—which in time may become familiar. Put simply, *UCAL* provides instruction in how to read certain contemporary writers—identifying and explicating their material, themes, use of language, point of view, structures, symbolism, and responses to experience.

The word *understanding* in the titles was deliberately chosen. Many willing readers lack an adequate understanding of how contemporary literature works; that is, what the author is attempting to express and the means by which it is conveyed. Although the criticism and analysis in the series have been aimed at a level of general accessibility, these introductory volumes are meant to be applied in conjunction with the works they cover. They do not provide a substitute for the works and authors they introduce, but rather prepare the reader for more profitable literary experiences.

M. J. B.

ACKNOWLEDGMENTS

I wish to acknowledge the advice, help, and support of the following, to each of whom I owe a debt of gratitude:

Roger Rawlings, Sheena Streather, and the staff at Liverpool John Moores University library, and the Kentucky Network, for providing me with primary research materials; Peter Nicholls, supervisor of my Ph.D. thesis, to whom I am indebted for his unfailing guidance and support in my initial work on Bobbie Ann Mason; Joe Moran, Colin Harrison, and Stephen Kenny, for their help in preparing the manuscript; and all those who have lent me their moral support during the period in which this book has come to fruition, especially Elspeth Graham, Edmund Cusick, Anne Clark, Toby Clark, June Price, and Pete Morriss.

CHAPTER ONE

Biography and Background

Bobbie Ann Mason's portrayal of small-town life in contemporary western Kentucky is rooted in her developing understanding of the cultural influences upon her own childhood and adolescence there. Mason was born on 1 May 1940 in Mayfield, Kentucky. The daughter of Wilburn Arnett Mason and Christianna Lee Mason and the eldest of four siblings, she grew up on the family dairy farm outside Mayfield. In these early years there was a close bond between family life and the land which has subsequently shaped the themes of Mason's fiction. To the young Mason, the farm was a "small universe, but rich," and there, learning about nature, she began to develop her keen eye for "physical details."[1]

After attending a small country school in the town of Cuba, Mason transferred to Mayfield High School, which she attended from 1954 to 1958. Here she experienced what she has called "a special kind of class difference" between town and country people. This "engendered feelings of inferiority in her" and was her first experience of the "culture shock" that has punctuated her life.[2] While at Mayfield High, Mason, a shy young woman, adapted to her feelings of isolation and difference from her classmates by immersion in various forms of popular culture. These also provided her with dreams of escape from farm and small-town life, an ambivalence toward which marks much of her work. From the age of ten, when a local drive-in theater was built, she would watch several movies a week.[3] She was also an avid reader of children's detective series fiction, the girl sleuths providing for her "my authorities, the source of my dreams."[4] These books inspired her, aged eleven, to write her first "novel," "The Carson Girls Go Abroad."[5] She shared with her parents a love of rock and roll, an enthusiasm that originated in their listening to black rhythm and blues from WLAC, Nashville, Tennessee, on the radio on Saturday nights in the 1950s.[6] Her interest in popular music, combined with her ambition to escape from small-town life, led the adolescent Mason to volunteer to start a fan club for the Hilltoppers. This band from Western Kentucky State College represented to Mason the possibility of leaving her local roots for a glamorous life of celebrity and travel. She showed precocious entrepreneurial flair as, holding the national office of president of the fan club, she published a bimonthly newsletter, was interviewed on the television and radio, and traveled to other states to report on the group.[7]

Popular culture both offered Mason images for her dreams of escape and was part of the world by which she felt circumscribed. She recounts how she spent the summer of 1958 picking blackberries, working in Rexall drugstore, and dating boys "who wanted to settle down and work in the new factories." Highway 45, which ran close to the Masons' farm "straight south to Tupelo, Mississippi, where Elvis was born," reminded Mason that "he had dreamed the same dreams" as she had.[8] Following her dreams, Mason went to the University of Kentucky in Lexington, where she started out as a math major in 1958 before switching to journalism and then to English, receiving her B.A.

in English literature in 1962. While a student, Mason pursued her interest in journalism, writing for the *Mayfield Messenger* during the summers and for the University of Kentucky *Kernel*. On graduating, she moved to New York to work for Ideal Publishing Company as a writer for fan magazines such as *Movie Stars, Movie Life,* and *TV Star Parade.* Although this work enabled her to pursue her interest in celebrity, Mason was still drawn to academia, and she left her job to take an M.A. in English literature at the State University of New York at Binghamton. After being awarded her M.A. in 1966, Mason attended graduate school at the University of Connecticut until 1971. She was awarded her Ph.D. for her dissertation on Vladimir Nabokov's novel *Ada* in 1972. This was published as *Nabokov's Garden: A Guide to Ada* in 1974. Mason's immediate reaction to her immersion in the rarefied air of "that wiley master of artifice," as she has described Nabokov, was to turn back to the children's detective series fiction which she had read in her childhood, to the popular culture which she believes "reflects our real desires and values" and "helps mold them."[9] Her study of this fiction was published as *The Girl Sleuth: A Feminist Guide to the Bobbsey Twins, Nancy Drew and Their Sisters* in 1975.

Mason married a fellow student, Roger Rawlings, in 1969, and two years later they moved to live on a farm in Mansfield, Pennsylvania. For several years Mason taught journalism part time at Mansfield State College. Throughout this period and her years at graduate school, Mason experimented with writing fiction, but she lacked the confidence to feel sure of her own subject matter. However, moving from the study of Nabokov to the memories evoked by her return to her own childhood reading enabled her to "realize a lot about where I'd come from, and then . . . to realize that that was the source of my experience and my material for my fiction."[10] In 1978 she stopped teaching to write full time and started submitting short stories to the *New Yorker.* Although her first story was rejected, she received a note of encouragement from one of the magazine's fiction editors, Roger Angell, and so continued to send more stories, each receiving helpful comments from Angell. After eighteen months her twentieth story, "Offerings," was accepted and published in 1980. "Shiloh" was published by the magazine later in the year. At this time, Mason also began contributing "Talk of the Town" articles to the *New Yorker.*

Mason's first collection of short stories, which had been previously published in such journals as the *Atlantic,* the *New Yorker, Bloodroot,* and *Redbook,* was published as *Shiloh and Other Stories* in 1982. The collection received immediate critical acclaim: it won the P.E.N./Hemingway Award and was a finalist for the National Book Critics Circle Award, the American Book Award, and the P.E.N./Faulkner Award. Her first novel, *In Country,* was published in 1985, receiving the President's Citation from the Vietnam Veterans of America, an award given to a non–Vietnam veteran who makes a significant contribution to the veterans' cause. In 1988 Mason published her second novel, *Spence + Lila,* and in 1989 she published her second collection of short stories, *Love Life.*

In 1990 Mason and her husband left southeast Pennsylvania, where they had moved in 1980, to live on a farm in central Kentucky. Mason's return to her cultural roots is reflected in her third novel, *Feather Crowns,* which was published in 1993, winning the Southern Book Award for Fiction. It was also a finalist for the National Book Critics Circle Award. In 1998 Mason published *Midnight Magic,* a selection of seventeen previously collected stories.

Mason's fiction is characterized by its distinctively economic but detailed representation of moments in the everyday life of mainly working-class characters in Kentucky from the 1970s to the present. The lives and thoughts of these characters are permeated by the images they encounter on television, in the movies, and through popular music. Critics have labeled Mason's short stories variously "K Mart realist," "dirty realist," "blue-collar minimalist hyper-realist," and "minimalist."[11] Mason herself, somewhat skeptical of such categorization, has wryly defined her fiction as "Southern Gothic Goes to the Supermarket."[12] Of these terms, the concepts of "dirty realism" and "minimalism" have the most critical currency. The term "dirty realism" was coined by Bill Buford to describe the type of writing included in two volumes of the British journal *Granta* that he edited under the titles *Dirty Realism: New Writing from America* and *More Dirt: New Writing from America.*[13] Contributors of stories to these volumes included Mason, Jayne Anne Phillips, Richard Ford, Raymond Carver, Elizabeth Tallent, Frederick Barthelme, and Tobias Wolff. These "dirty realists," who emerged in the 1980s, were partly reacting against the "metafiction" of the 1960s and 1970s, which drew attention to the way meaning is constructed through the relations between the writer, reader, and text. Their writing, however, does not seek to return to an unselfconscious realism. As they represent identity in consumer culture, these writers modify conventional realism. The dominant narratives of realism, in particular those of a linear "History" underpinning a chronological narrative, and those of gender, home, and community are present in these texts, but they are accompanied by an often ironic reflexivity. These writings are woven out of allusions to the images and objects of popular culture: they frequently have a soundtrack of popular music from the 1960s through the 1980s, and they make constant references to brand names, television programs, and mass media personalities. In the stories the main consensus that the characters hold about a shared reality is drawn from the interpretations of everyday life offered by popular cultural narratives, particularly as shaped by television.

The works of the dirty realists are marked by a sense of the lost idealism and optimism of the 1960s, which is associated with the countercultural vision of alternative possibilities to those offered by consumerism. The effect of these years is often felt by their characters who, in the late 1970s or 1980s, either remain rootless wanderers or else feel an unarticulated dissatisfaction with lives predominantly defined by consumer culture. A sense of loss pervades the lives of the characters in these stories. This is most acutely felt within the family, which is typically riven by separation, divorce, bereavement, and estrangement between the sexes and the generations.

Loss is also inscribed in the distinctive style of the dirty realists. As Bill Buford has remarked, this writing is at once "stylized and particularized" and "flat" and "'unsurprised' . . . pared down to the plainest of plain styles."[14] Through this honed-down style, he observes, "it's what's not being said—the silences, the elisions, the omissions—that seem to speak most."[15] These writers, drawing upon the conventions of both realism and the short story, use a small scene, a typical detail, to offer a glimpse into a whole culture. Often what is typified appears to be the withering of remembered social structures, as the characters become increasingly isolated, their relations to others always mediated by commodities or television images.

Critics have also appropriated the term "minimalism" to denote contemporary writing such as Mason's that is economic, literal, and focused upon mundane details, and that leaves the reader to infer meaning from what is unsaid. Moreover, they have argued that the "minimalist" style communicates an essentially pessimistic and passive view of the world.[16] As Barbara Henning has suggested, Mason's honed-down style, which concentrates "on the literal detail" and which generally lacks "metaphoric depth," effectively evokes the way in which her characters "survive . . . in a world with reduced economic and emotional possibilities" by displacing their anxieties through "a steady focus on the random details of everyday life."[17] Yet the presence of figurative patterns in Mason's texts allows the reader the possibility of making connections that ameliorate the apparent randomness of the lives being represented.

Although the similarities between Mason's work and that of some of her contemporaries place it within a particular literary milieu, her style cannot be attributed to the direct influence of an individual writer or school of writing. Rather, Mason's distinctive style and themes are the product of her recognition of specific cultural conjunctions in her own life and education. One such conjunction, which greatly influenced her choice of subject matter and the style she was to craft, was her transition from writing her doctoral study of Nabokov's *Ada* to rereading the detective series fiction she had enjoyed in her childhood. Mason was particularly interested in Nabokov's craft as a stylist,[18] and the evolution of her own aesthetics can be discerned in the limpid and sympathetic reading of *Ada* she offers in *Nabokov's Garden.* In *Ada* Nabokov presents the "Family Chronicle" through which his narrator, Van Veen, re-creates Ardis, the "Eden" of his childhood. At the center of this Eden are Van Veen's incestuous relations with his sister Ada and half-sister, Lucette. Though his writing, with its falsification of memory, Van Veen tries to preserve his relation with Ada. Van Veen's solipsistic chronicle is written in the luxuriant language typical of Nabokov's narrators. Crucial to Mason's reading of the novel is her emphasis on the distinction, sustained by authorial irony, between the destructive desires that Van Veen expresses through his decadent language and the life-affirming point of view that Nabokov communicates through his authorial precision. Mason commends the authorial virtues of distance, control, reflexivity, and discernment that are communicated through Nabokov's precise attention to detail. She observes that it was Nabokov's artistic credo "the detail is all" that enabled him to create: "the texture of artistic perceptions which, to my mind, emerges as the most enduring facet of [his] art—the delicate caressing of fine pinpoint perceptions which gain precedence over more 'profound' or 'moral' truths."[19] In her own fiction Mason was to take these aspects of Nabokov's style as her model, striving to create a controlled but compassionate representation of "reality" through a close rendering of details.

The modernist precepts of authorial control and narrative detach-ment have remained important elements of her craft, despite her insistence in interviews on the relative spontaneity of her writing methods.[20]

Mason's initial reaction to the self-absorbed aesthetics of Van Veen and more generally to her own years of studying Nabokov's work was to reject the modernist elevation of art over life and what she regarded as the elitism and insularity of acade-mia.[21] In her next book, *The Girl Sleuth,* Mason offers a cultural study of the development of detective series books for children, focusing particularly on the figure of the girl sleuth. She traces a tension in the representation of this figure between stereotypes of femininity that circumscribe possibilities for their girl readers and a vision of freedom through adventure that had not been available to these readers elsewhere. She was to return to explore this tension between "femininity" and freedom in several of her short stories and, more fully, as a central theme of *In Country* and *Feather Crowns.* Notably, Mason's valuing of these books represents her renewed embrace of the popular culture that had been important to her in her childhood. In her preface to *The Girl Sleuth,* she defends the study of this popular fiction as one that "acknowledges significant textures of our real (if sometimes embarrassedly hidden) lives" and that "helps us to discover who we really are—an essential prerequisite to deciding who we want to become."[22] The importance of the cultural and aesthetic values that clarified for Mason through her work on *The Girl Sleuth* were a development of those she had already begun to formulate through her reading of *Ada.*

In *Nabokov's Garden* Mason had criticized the "inauthenticity" of the decadent, densely metaphoric language of Van Veen, Nabokov's narrator.[23] In the preface to *The Girl Sleuth,* she observes wryly that in graduate school, "we didn't talk about actual trees and cats, but only metaphorical ones."[24] At this point Mason was coming to value a literal language grounded in the observation of concrete details rather than an ostentatiously metaphoric one that, in *Ada,* had been associated with a solipsistic retreat from the world. Significantly for the choice Mason was also to make at this time of what was to be her subject matter, this developing aesthetics was becoming connected with her recognition of the importance to her of the culture of her childhood. One of the effects of this recognition was a sharpened appreciation of the language spoken by the people with whom she grew up in Kentucky. She has explained that "my language derives from the language of farm life which is very practical and not decorative."[25] This is her mother's language, Mason has commented, and it is rooted in the memories and traditions of a community.[26] In "The Way We Lived: The Chicken Tower," an article about changing ways of life in rural Kentucky, Mason commented that "my mother uses idioms that are dying out with her generation, right along with the small family farms of America. Her way of talking is the most familiar thing I know, except maybe for the contours and textures of this land."[27] Embedded in Mason's characters' colloquialisms, she notes, are metaphors that retain their vitality because they draw upon common knowledge and memory.[28]

Mason has observed that the contrast between the plain speech of her immediate childhood community and the language of polite Southern society embodied a "class distinction."[29] Elsewhere she has remarked that although she is not particularly concerned with "politics," she has become increasingly preoccupied with "the class struggle."[30] In interviews Mason has expressed a feeling of affinity with Nabokov because "he was an exile and he had two opposing cultures in his head, Russia and America, and in my own way I feel a similar sort of schizophrenia with the North and South."[31] The sense of "exile" she experienced on attending graduate school and living in the North related to a "class difference," she has explained: that created by Southerners' sense of cultural and historical inferiority to Northerners.[32] Mason has also attributed the experience of culture shock consequent upon being an exile to Mark Twain, whose fiction she holds in high regard.[33] The culture shock that accompanied Twain's move from Missouri to New York State, Mason proposes, was "the most significant split" to influence "the contradictions and paradoxes" in his life and writing.[34] Moreover, as in the case of Nabokov, Mason relates this clash of cultures to the qualities of Twain's writing that she admires. She suggests that the "deepest source of [Twain's] artistic energy" was the "rigged-up language" of his boyhood, which had a "potential for inventiveness just as the necessities of the frontier called for ingenious solutions."[35] As in her own fiction, Twain's style, according to Mason, also revealed a class difference: the "plain style" through which he "emphasized the dignity and complexity of people often dismissed as illiterate" "deflowered" the "literary language" favored by educated readers at the end of the nineteenth century.

Mason has also applied the concepts of exile and of "culture shock" that this produces to the characters in her fiction, specifically to "people moving from one class to another" and those whose values are challenged by the television, or when they leave home.[36] Mason's growing sense of the significance of class difference affected her choice of the characters about whom she would write: she has reiterated that she was tired of reading "about the alienated hero of a superior sensibility" whom she found in Nabokov's fiction and that has also provided the dominant narrative consciousness in canonical American literature.[37] She identifies her own work with the "shift of emphasis away from the hero leaving society to the hero trying to get into the mainstream . . . a shift of emphasis away . . . from an enlightened guy who is sort of an artist figure to the little guy."[38]

Mason's characters, many of whom have their origins in the rural poor, are mostly working class or in low-level white-collar jobs. But they also belong to a new and growing class of Americans whose consciousness is shaped by the images and ideology of consumer culture, as disseminated by television, movies, and to a lesser extent, radio. These images, as purveyed by advertising and popular music, for example, dictate how Mason's characters are to spend their leisure time, what defines their taste, and, more generally, what will constitute their happiness. Mason explores the effect upon her characters of the "democratizing" discourses that are transmitted through the popular media. In her fiction the most influential of these discourses about the possibility of attaining new freedoms, rights, and empowerment are those of feminism and formal education. As appropriated by consumer culture, the main means of attaining the abstract goals represented by these discourses is through increased consumer choice and the commodities that this makes available. The "dizzying" choices with which her characters are faced is one of Mason's recurring themes. She explores the way in which the proliferation of choices promises her characters more autonomy and responsibility for their own lives, while also producing in them a sense of anxiety and a feeling of not being fully in control.[39] Hence Mason's characters exist in "a kind of affective democracy, with feelings of anxiety cutting across economic setting," as Duncan Webster has put it.[40]

As these discourses about the pursuit of freedom and equality are translated by consumer culture and understood by Mason's characters, they incorporate the reworking of an old American myth: the American Dream, with its attendant notions of the attainment of progress and individualism through the acquisition of wealth and social status. Mason has stated that she regards the persistence of the American Dream, as exemplified by many of her characters' embrace of "progress," as cause for optimism.[41] Yet one of her recurrent themes is the conflict between the desires to cling to the past or to embrace the future. She relates this to her characters' ambivalence toward notions of "home," torn as many of them are between seeking it and desiring to escape from it. Variations on the theme of how to adapt to change recur throughout Mason's stories as her characters must choose between staying at home, leaving, or returning; taking risks or avoiding them; holding on or letting go.[42] The uncertainty produced by these choices is reflected in the structure of the stories, which are open-ended, leaving the reader to decide whether to seek resolution in their concluding images.

A related theme of Mason's work is the multifaceted sense of loss experienced by her characters. Her work can be read as recording the "Americanization" of her characters and of the South through the cultural homogenization effected by consumer culture. But in doing so, it also documents some of the changes occurring in contemporary Kentucky. Foremost among these changes is that of a rural society with an agrarian economy into a consumer-based society. Land ownership has been centralized through the transfer of small, family-owned farms to corporate ownership,[43] and the landscape has been transformed by freeways, subdivisions, shopping malls, television, and telephones. The nature of labor and the use of time has also changed: most of Mason's characters are in impermanent jobs and spend their increased leisure time in pursuits such as shopping, driving, and watching television. Many of them also feel that their knowledge, which may have seemed secure in its relation to their labor or the land, now seems invalid as they are saturated by new information through the mass media. Mason explores how, with the loss of many of the traditions associated with a central relation to the land, people must redefine such fundamental concepts as those of home, community, and self.[44]

Mason's fiction is consistently concerned with the ways in which ideas of self have been affected by the alteration of gender roles and the relation between the sexes over the past few decades. However, when questioned about feminism, a significant catalyst of this change, Mason has been circumspect about its influence upon her own thought. She has explained that although she "went through the compulsory stage of feminism," she "internalized feminism and figured out where my experience fit into the whole thing," and then " it was time to move on."[45] Mason's "internalization" of feminist discourse is revealed in the

attentiveness of her fiction to the effects of changing gender formations. For her characters, however, the effects of a feminism
that has reached them piecemeal through the channels of the
mass media are less well understood. For her women characters,
the assimilation of feminist ideas manifests itself mainly in the
desire for more personal autonomy, whether this be through the
questioning of a marriage or other relationship, exercising more
control over their bodies and sexuality, or seeking increased freedom and knowledge through education and travel.[46] Mason has
suggested that although for the women she portrays these
choices may produce anxiety and be accompanied by the loss of
former certainties about their social role, some sense of empowerment is generally an element of the women's response to them.
She has explained that she is "more interested in the cultural
effects [of feminism] on men" and how they are adapting to the
alteration of their roles and women's.[47] This interest is reflected
in her stories, many of which focus on male protagonists who are
experiencing such changes as unemployment and the loss of the
role of breadwinner, a sense of inadequate education and a
bewilderment about women's changing expectations of themselves and men.

The alteration of gender roles and of relations between the
sexes is one of the main elements of the changes to the family
unit in the society that Mason depicts: here, nuclear and extended
families are being replaced by more temporary relations. This
fluidity is increased by the geographical dispersal of family
members and an estrangement between the generations that,
while not being new, has been accelerated by recent cultural
shifts. The changing structure of the family is part of a larger

alteration of traditional notions of community associated with shared labor and a common relation to the land. This sense of community would have been cemented by common rituals, but in the contemporary society depicted by Mason, characters must improvise their own rituals. These tend to be provisional and solitary and are often dictated by a consumer culture that confers upon them only an ephemeral significance.[48] However, Mason's fiction suggests that a new commonality is being forged by people's shared experience of the images and ideas disseminated by the mass media, although this is paradoxically a community in which the individual feels isolated by his or her distance from its other members. Many of her characters attempt to use these images to interpret their own lives and connect them to larger cultural changes.[49]

An important theme of Mason's work is the way in which traditional notions of community have been eroded by the loss of collective memories. Part of the anxiety experienced by Mason's characters originates in their sense of disconnection from history and their powerlessness to affect any social changes that are shaping their lives. In an influential essay, "Postmodernism and Consumer Society," Fredric Jameson has argued that contemporary (American) society is undergoing a "disappearance of a sense of history" and the gradual loss of "its capacity to retain its own past," with the effect that its subjects have "begun to live in a perpetual present and in a perpetual change that obliterates traditions of the kind which all earlier social formations have had in one way or another to preserve."[50] One of the main causes of this "historical amnesia,"[51] according to Jameson, is the mass media, particularly television, which converts all references to the past into barely connected images or sound bites to be rapidly consumed by a generic "channel-switching"[52] viewer. These fragmentary images do not allow the viewer to create, and connect him- or herself to, a meaningful narrative or interpretation that links past, present, and future.

Critics of fiction such as Mason's, particularly those who regard it as "minimalist," have argued that it maintains a restrictive focus on the suspension of its characters in the present moment. Like Jameson, these critics have attributed this choice of focus largely to the authors' perception of the effect of television both on the characters and on readers, in that "in the TV age of shortened attention spans, perhaps the main challenge of writing is keeping a reader's interest."[53] Robert Dunn, for example, writing of what he terms "private-interest fiction," has asked scathingly: "What can we expect from a collective memory that responds to the brief vagaries and vicissitudes of media attention, that finds its common material in trivia about old movies and television programs?"[54]

According to such critics, in order to realistically evoke their characters' sense of disconnection from history, as well as to appeal to the diminished attention span of their readers, writers such as Mason use devices such as setting their stories in the present tense, with frequent dialogue and "scenes," and concentrating on "the impartial observation of detail," all of which relieve the author of the burden of "exegesis."[55] The perceived effect of such devices is that not only do the characters lack an historical consciousness, but the fiction itself fails to evince an "historical sense" that would interpret the present through reflection on the past and a vision of the future.[56] This effect is intensified by the fact that the short story, as Andrew Levy has observed, is a "present-oriented" literary form that "has been designed as a culturally disposable artifact—a thing to be read once and enjoyed."[57] Levy explains that the impression a short story creates upon the reader depends upon a "unity" that is "the result of an uninterrupted engagement with the text."[58] In Mason's fiction this "throwaway effect"[59] is compounded by the density of popular cultural references, which, some critics fear, may render the texts as rapidly obsolete as the products to which they refer.[60]

Yet Mason's fiction, in particular the novel *In Country,* may also be read as offering an exploration of the way in which popular cultural forms, such as pop songs and television programs, can be used to stimulate an active engagement with the past. Mason identifies the 1960s and 1970s as the defining historical moment for the characters of her short stories and *In Country,* although she does not return to the watershed in Southern history constituted by events surrounding race relations and the civil rights movement in this period.[61] Much of her fiction explores the effect on her characters of other changes that occurred in this period, particularly as a result of the war in Vietnam, but also due to the emergence of the countercultural discourses that offered a vision of alternative values and ways of life. Her characters often experience a loss of stability resulting from the challenges that arose in this period to authoritative and consolatory narratives. The way in which the sense of loss that permeates contemporary American society has become part of a cultural process of mourning is the central theme of *In Country.* Yet Mason's fiction, which rarely succumbs to nostalgia, also expresses a sense of optimism about the continued possibility of embracing change.

CHAPTER TWO

Shiloh and Other Stories

Mason's first collection of short stories, *Shiloh and Other Stories,* was generally well-received by critics. Robert Towers observed that Mason "is one of those rare writers who, by concentrating their attention on a few square miles of native turf, are able to open up new and surprisingly wide worlds for the delighted reader."[1] Anne Tyler recognized Mason as already "a full-fledged master of the short story." Tyler applauded Mason's compassionate treatment of her characters who, although feeling "bewilderment" at the changes that confront them, nevertheless try to adapt to them with an "optimistic faith in progress."[2] Tyler observed that "it is especially poignant that the characters in these stories, having led more sheltered lives than the average reader, are trying to deal with changes that most of us already take for granted."[3] Mason herself has reflected that the "strength of my fiction has been the tension between being from there and not from there"[4] and has commented that "My work seems to have struck a chord with a number of readers who have left home and maybe who have rejected it, and I think it startles them because they thought they were rid of it."[5] Andrew Levy points out that in Mason's own view, the appeal of her stories to the lower-upper-class or upper-middle-class readership of such magazines as the *New Yorker* lies in the fact that "reading her stories, like writing them, constitutes an act of reconciliation with the home that is left behind."[6] Moreover, Levy continues, "the 'home' that is left behind is not just rural

Kentucky, but the popular culture that is repudiated (or diluted) by a rising middle class, or an entrenched upper class." According to Levy, Mason's stories, therefore, appeal to an audience that is largely "displaced out of its class of origin" through the "reconciliation" of class differences that they represent.[7]

Other reviewers argued that the stories in *Shiloh* epitomized the limitations of "minimalist" writing. Robert Dunn, for example, commented that the stories are an example of "private interest fiction" in that their characters, lacking a sense of history, focus their anxieties about cultural change exclusively through a diminished world of private relationships.[8] Similarly, John Barth and Ben Yagoda, while recognizing that this fiction aspires to give a realistic representation of a consumer culture dominated by television, lamented its perceived failure to offer a broader, historicized interpretation of that culture.[9] Yagoda concluded that writers of such fiction, including Mason, "give us random and unimaginatively chosen details and events, signifying nothing."[10]

As the reviewers observed, the most initially striking quality of the short stories collected in *Shiloh* is Mason's evocative rendering of the details of the daily lives of her characters. The central theme of the stories is the way in which Mason's characters respond to the changes effected by contemporary culture on formerly rural life in western Kentucky. Mason generally renders the narrative perspective on these changes either through a working-class character who is trying to adjust to the cultural shifts through which he or she is living or through an educated, newly middle-class woman character who is reflecting on some of the changes in order to interpret her past and present life.

The thematic coherence of the collection as a whole is underpinned by two of the stories, "Residents and Transients" and "Shiloh." "Residents and Transients" is the first-person narrative of Mary, who has returned to her childhood home in Kentucky after spending eight years away, "pursuing higher learning."[11] Those closest to Mary have embraced change: her parents have moved to Florida, and her husband has moved to Louisville, expecting his wife to follow. Due to the years Mary has spent away from "home," married to a "Yankee," she now feels like an exile even when she is there. She seeks stability in her parents' farm and particularly the remembered rituals of the canning room. As she recalls time spent with her lover, Larry, a local dentist, Mary's increasing anxiety about her own identity and her sense of paralysis before the choices confronting her become apparent. She tries to remind herself of who she is by itemizing the components of her identity: "I am nearly thirty years old. I have two men, eight cats, no cavities" (127). But her world appears to be dissolving as her husband, who is "processing words" over the telephone, makes her "think of liquidity, investment postures. I see him floppy as Raggedy Andy, loose as a goose" (131). Mary's dissociation both from her husband's words and values and from herself is reflected in her observation that "I see what I am shredding in my hand as I listen. It is Monopoly money" (131).

As Mary and her lover drive back toward the farm at night, she sees "a rabbit move. It is hopping in place, the way runners will run in place. Its forelegs are frantically working, but its rear end has been smashed and it cannot get out of the road" (130). To Mary the rabbit becomes "a tape loop that crowds out everything else," like Stephen's words, which liquefy in her mind. To the reader the rabbit may serve as a metaphor for Mary's own immobilization. In this story, as in others, Mason weaves in images that may be used by the reader to interpret the unfolding narrative.

Here, more unusually, the metaphoric potential of the images is apparent to the story's narrator, which enables her to approach an interpretation of her situation and from this to take some control over the choices that confront her. Mary explains to Larry: "In the wild, there are two kinds of cat populations . . . Residents and transients. Some stay put, in their fixed home ranges, and others are on the move. They don't have real homes. Everybody always thought that the ones who establish territories are the most successful . . . They are the strongest, while the transients are the bums, the losers." But, she continues, "it may be that the transients are the superior ones after all, with the greatest curiosity and most intelligence" (128–9). The image of residents and transients resonates throughout the collection as a metaphor for Mason's characters' ambivalence toward "home." By analogy with this information about cats, Mary is able to reflect upon her own indecision about whether to stay at home or to leave. The final image of the story is typical of Mason's concluding images in its ambiguity. It evokes Mary's new receptiveness to change, but she is still watching herself waiting, rather than acting: "I see a cat's flaming eyes coming up the lane to the house. One eye is green and one is red, like a traffic light. . . . In a moment I realize that I am waiting for the light to change" (131).

The theme of the conflict between the desires to stay at

home, to leave, or to return; to recover the past or to forget it; to "let go" or to seek safety in "hanging on" is established in the first story, "Shiloh." The wide anthologization and extensive critical study of this story attest to Mason's consummate achievement of a style that imitates the content of the story, as her representation of her characters' responses to change offers penetrating insights into their culture. Mason's sympathetic evocation of Leroy Moffitt exemplifies her compassionate interest in men who are struggling to adapt to changes that their women relatives or partners are finding at least partially empowering. Leroy is a truck driver who is unemployed after an accident has left him with a limp. Forced to give up his life on the road, Leroy observes with a sense of bewildered helplessness and fear the changes taking place in his hometown, his wife, and his marriage. Mason succinctly evokes Leroy's perception of the destructiveness of these changes in one simile: "Subdivisions are spreading across western Kentucky like an oil slick" (3). Terry Thompson has pointed out that "a subdivision is, first of all, a 'backwards' community: it is built on speculation *before* there are people to populate it." Thompson glosses Mason's simile accordingly: "one could argue, oil spills are eventually cleaned up, but subdivisions continue to devour valuable farmland that could grow corn or wheat instead of sprouting generic ranch houses with generic mortgages and synthetic neighbors."[12] As Leroy drives to a new shopping center, he realizes that the repopulation of the landscape has occurred through the erosion of the old economy and community as he remembered it: "The farmers who used to gather around the courthouse square on Saturday afternoons to play checkers and spit tobacco juice have gone. It has been years since Leroy has thought about the farmers, and they have disappeared without his noticing" (4). Leroy's nostalgia for the security of a simpler past is manifested in his making "things from craft kits," beginning by "building a miniature log cabin from notched Popsicle sticks" that "reminds him of a rustic Nativity scene" (1). His hobby develops into a dream of building a log cabin as a home for himself and his wife, Norma Jean. This fantasy shows the value that the unemployed Leroy places on craftsmanship in the homogenized landscape of shopping malls and subdivisions and how he has turned to the American dream of self-reliance in a society to which he feels he has become superfluous.

The Moffitts' responses to change are differentiated along gender lines. Norma Jean has assimilated fragments of feminist discourse to forge her own American dream of progress as she seeks personal autonomy through further education, going to night school at Paducah Community College. She has also taken up bodybuilding, Leroy having introduced her to weights through the physical therapy he is doing to build up his weakened body. As, with Leroy, the reader watches Norma Jean "working on her pectorals," she seems a testimony to consumer culture's dictum that to re-create the body is to reinvent the self. The apparent reversal of gender roles is provocatively commented upon by Norma Jean's mother, Mabel, who, observing Leroy's needlepoint, remarks: "That's what a woman would do" (6). Norma Jean's self-education is also producing signs of an emergent class difference between herself and her husband, as is suggested, for example, by Leroy's observation that "Recently Norma Jean has been cooking unusual food—tacos, lasagna, Bombay chicken" (11).

Leroy watches these changes in his wife apprehensively, realizing that "something is happening" and knowing "he is going to lose her" (11). He recognizes that in the years he spent on the road, "he was always flying past scenery" (2) and that in order to understand what is happening to him in the present, he must stop and reflect on the past. The loss of their son, Randy, by sudden infant death syndrome, several years ago is a fault line running through the Moffitts' marriage. They do not ever speak of this loss, although Leroy, deriving his knowledge from popular culture, "has read that for most people losing a child destroys the marriage—or else he heard this on *Donahue*" (3). Leroy, trying to recover some truth in memory, finds that he "can hardly remember the child anymore" but that he recalls vividly "a scene from *Dr. Strangelove*," which the couple were watching at a drive-in when the child died in their car. The film serves as a displacement of too painful a memory. Mason evokes how images from the film became "facts" for Leroy while the emotional "truth" of the situation evaded him, such that he fantasized that the hospital was the "War Room" of *Dr. Strangelove* while wondering of his wife: "Who is this strange girl? He had forgotten who she was" (5). The shock of his sudden bereavement reverberates through the culture shock Leroy experiences later as he registers the cultural dislocations that are fracturing his marriage. Here, too, an involuntary forgetting protects Leroy from the painfulness of what memory may reveal: he resolves "to tell

Norma Jean about himself, as if he had just met her," but instantly "he forgets why he wants to do this" (9).

Observing his present situation, Leroy continues to look aslant rather than directly at the cause of his unhappiness, as for example in this passage: "He sees things about Norma Jean that he never realized before. When she chops onions, she stares off into a corner, as if she can't bear to look. She puts on her house slippers almost precisely at nine o'clock every evening and nudges her jogging shoes under the couch. She saves bread heels for the birds. Leroy watches the birds at the feeder. He notices the peculiar way goldfinches fly past the window. They close their wings, then fall, then spread their wings to catch and lift themselves. He wonders if they close their eyes when they fall. Norma Jean closes her eyes when they are in bed. She wants the lights turned out. Even then, he is sure she closes her eyes" (7). Norma Jean's averted gaze as she chops onions is paralleled by Leroy's: he can observe the literal details of her domestic rituals but will not pursue his observations further in order to reach an understanding of her behavior that may offer some insight into their relationship. Mason's mimetic representation of Leroy's small, self-contained observations through pared-down, clipped sentences could be read as an example of that minimalist writing that confines itself to the local detail, refusing to take any greater burden of interpretative authority for what is represented. On the other hand, it may be read as the effective exercise of the authorial control Mason had admired in Nabokov's writing, whereby "pain or grief becomes suggestively more intense because it is in the process of being toned down from raging torrents of tears and shrieks of pain. Authorial distance saves it from sentimentality and also makes it bearable for the reader."[13] It is through such authorial control that Mason is able to sustain a fine, ironic distance between her character's perception and her reader's. She creates for the reader the possibility of an interpretation that exceeds that of her characters while retaining consistency in her representation of the character's point of view. The return of Leroy's thoughts to Norma Jean after an apparently whimsical reflection on the flight of the goldfinches suggests his anguished desire to be certain that he still knows who his wife is. Leroy, who clings to facts and literal details, does not draw any conscious analogy between the falling goldfinches and his own feelings about himself and Norma Jean. For the reader, however, the goldfinches as they "close their wings, then fall, then spread their wings to catch and lift themselves" hover as a possible metaphor for either Leroy, trying to protect himself against change, or Norma Jean, who may be "falling" as she prepares to take flight. Characteristically, interpretation remains suspended as authorial resolution is withheld throughout.[14]

Leroy is prompted not by his own memory but by that of his mother-in-law to visit Shiloh with Norma Jean. Leroy, for whom the present has become evacuated of history, anticipates that this National Historical Site, the Civil War battleground in Tennessee, "would look like a golf course." He tries to impress Norma Jean and to dull his own pain with disconnected facts about the battle, but "they both know that he doesn't know any history" (14). Mason describes how, as Leroy hears Norma Jean telling him she wants to leave him, his gaze takes in the Shiloh cemetery. Mason's setting of this dialogue at the scene of "that darkest place in Southern history, where 24,000 soldiers were wounded, and 3,500 of them died in battle,"[15] invites the reader to reflect on the legacy of the past, and specifically on the effect on the Moffitts' marriage of their inability to mourn together their own dead. But for Leroy the unconfronted past returns to the literal details of a barely interpreted present: "The cemetery, a green slope dotted with white markers, looks like a subdivision site. Leroy is trying to comprehend that his marriage is breaking up, but for some reason he is wondering about white slabs in a graveyard" (15). However, as he tries to form a narrative that connects random facts about the battle to the marriage of his parents-in-law and to his own marriage, Leroy approaches an epiphany precisely in his recognition that "he is leaving out a lot. He is leaving out the insides of history. History was always just names and dates to him. It occurs to him that building a house out of logs is similarly empty—too simple. And the real inner workings of a marriage, like most of history, have escaped him" (16).

The outcome of Leroy's revelation is left inconclusive. The closing image sequence presents Leroy trying to "hobble toward" a distant Norma Jean. With poignant humor that hesitates between the metaphoric and the literal, the revelatory and the banal, Mason describes how Norma Jean turns toward Leroy "and waves her arms. Is she beckoning him? She seems to be doing an exercise for her chest muscles. The sky is unusually pale—the color of the dust ruffle Mabel made for their bed" (16). Through these concluding images, Mason evokes both the ambiguity of Norma Jean's gesture and the irresolution of Leroy's response to it. His observation that "the sky is unusually pale" suggests how for Leroy, in his shock, the world has become drained of color, while Mason's final, flattened image of the "dust-ruffle" evokes Leroy's desire to avert pain by returning his perception to the familiar and domestic detail. At the same time, the selection of this particular detail is also inscribed with his sense of loss. Through these images Mason sustains a delicate equilibrium between the possibility that Leroy is recognizing that loss or that he is denying it.

In the next story, "The Rookers," Mason again explores her characters' responses to "culture shock," sustaining her sympathetic focus on the apprehensive response to change of a male character, Mack Skaggs. Change is most acutely felt by Mary Lou and Mack Skaggs through the dispersal of their family, particularly through the departure of their youngest daughter for college. In her daughter's absence, Mary Lou enjoys a new ritualized connection through her meetings with her widowed friends to play Rook. She is also adjusting to popular culture, enjoying an "R-rated movie," for example. She observes how her husband, however, whom "the highway . . . makes nervous," is retreating into the security of his carpentry workshop. Like Leroy Moffitt, Mack Skaggs is trying to create order in a changing world through craftsmanship. Mary Lou observes how the card table that Mack has made out of pieces of scrap pine seems to express his desire to form a whole out of the fragments of his life: "It seemed that Mack was trying to put together the years of their marriage into a convincing whole and this was as far as he got" (18). Mack retreats further from the workshop in his basement to the television in his den. From the safety of his home, Mack tries to adjust to the changes that are invading it by reading the books that he believes his daughter Judy is studying. Judy's attempt to explain quantum mechanics to her parents provides the central metaphor of the story: "'If you separate them [photons], they disappear. They don't even *exist* except in a group'" (27). Shortly afterward, Mary Lou reflects: "If you break up a group, the individuals could disappear out of existence." She is afraid that her husband "is disappearing like that, disconnected from everybody" (29). This metaphor resonates throughout the collection of stories, evoking the characters' fear as they feel themselves becoming increasingly isolated as familiar social structures appear to disintegrate. Mack Skaggs tries to both forge a controlled connection with the world outside his home and to regulate the information entering it, undermining former certainties, by constantly calling the weather report on the telephone. The story concludes with Mary Lou's realization that "Mack calls the temperature number because he is afraid to talk on the telephone, and by listening to a recording, he doesn't have to reply. It's his way of pretending that he's involved. He wants it to snow so that he won't have to go outside. He is afraid of what might happen." Mary Lou continues to reflect that what her husband "must really be afraid of is women," which makes her feel "so sick and heavy with her power over him that she wants to cry" (33). This unexpected shift in the narrative's exploration of change aligns the story with "Shiloh" and others in the collection, implicitly identifying the recent alteration of gender roles as perhaps the most powerful cause of cultural dislocation. The final image is of Mack standing "in a frozen pose," paralyzed by the changes that invade his household.

Mason explores the effect of contemporary cultural shifts on family life in three other stories, "Old Things," "Drawing Names," and "Graveyard Day." In "Old Things" Cleo Watkins has to some extent accepted personal change, selling her farm, moving to a new house in town, and giving away reminders of her deceased husband. She is distressed, however, by her daughter's arrival with her two children after she has left her husband. While her daughter tells Cleo that "you could go to school, make a nurse," Cleo tries to instill in her daughter traditional values with such advice as "a man takes care of a woman" (80). To Cleo her daughter's tales of her marital breakdown seem as strange as though "she has been told some wild tale about outer space, like something on a TV show" (80). The story depicts Cleo trying to reconcile what she felt to be a harmonious past rooted in traditional family values with a rapidly changing present, in order to imagine an acceptable future. Yet she does not believe that the past can be repossessed through the current fashion for commodifying former ways of life. She has no sympathy with her daughter's taste for "antiquing" the "paraphernalia" of farm life and is shocked when she sees farmers selling now unused farm objects at a local market.

At the end of the story, however, she finds at the market "a miniature Early American whatnot" that she recognizes as one she had given away. The picture on the whatnot of "a train running through a meadow" stimulates a reverie that provides the concluding images of the story. Cleo imagines the train "gliding . . . out West" with her remaining family aboard: "Cleo is following unafraid in the caboose, as the train passes through the golden meadow and they all wave at the future and smile perfect smiles" (93). These images are ambiguous in their evocation of a fantasy of the future based on the projection of a nostalgic longing for the past, which denies change and the disharmony that it has produced. Yet at the same time they, like Cleo's purchase of the whatnot, suggest that she can become more accepting of a recent past about which she has felt some guilt, having believed that her husband "would never forgive her for selling the farm" (90).

In "Graveyard Day," which was included in *Best American Short Stories of 1983* and *Pushcart Prize VIII: Best of the Small Presses,* Mason again explores the effect of cultural changes upon shifting family relationships. The story traces the increasing anxiety of Waldeen, whose ex-husband has left for Arizona. Waldeen reflects that if she were to marry her new lover, Joe McClain, her daughter would have a stepfather, "something like a sugar substitute," but, Waldeen feels, "families shouldn't shift memberships, like clubs. But here they are, trying to be a family" (167). Waldeen is also sensitive to other changes, wrought largely through the influx of new ideas, which make themselves felt through generational differences. This is evident even in that most domestic of rituals, preparing food: while "Waldeen is tenderizing liver. . . . Her daughter insists that she is a vegetarian. If Holly had said Rosicrucian it would have sounded just as strange to Waldeen" (165).

In this story, however, unusually in the increasingly "Americanized" South evoked by Mason, tradition has been preserved through a particular ritual: Joe McClain tells Waldeen how each spring he maintains a family ritual by raking over his grandparents' grave and placing geraniums there. Waldeen suggests that she and her daughter accompany Joe on a picnic to the graveyard while he undertakes this ritual. As in "Shiloh," a visit to a grave-yard allows the characters to reflect on the losses borne in con-temporary cultural changes. Waldeen's anxiety is manifested in her increasing morbidity throughout this scene. Approaching the graveyard, she compares Joe's geraniums to "a petrified Easter basket" and imagines "that they were in a funeral procession" (174). Thoughts of love, marriage, and death merge as Waldeen imagines that "the burial plot, not a diamond ring, symbolizes the promise of marriage" (177).

Whereas in "Shiloh," however, Leroy and Norma Jean Mof-fitt lack a ritual through which to acknowledge and mourn together the loss of their son and the disintegration of their mar-riage, Waldeen's observation of Joe's continuance of a family ritual seems to help her to begin to cohere the fragments that she feels constitute her life. The morbid analogies she has been nur-turing give way to a memory of being on a pedal boat on a lake with a former boyfriend. As they had spent the entire afternoon there, her boyfriend had "worked Saturdays . . . to pay for their spree." Waldeen recalls that in a recent encounter, he had told her that "it was worth it, for it was one of the great adventures of his life, going out on a pedal boat with Waldeen, with nothing but the lake and time" (177–8). This memory leads to the con-cluding images of the narrative: "Waldeen has pulled her shoes off. Then she is taking a long running start, like a pole vaulter, and then with a flying leap she lands in the immense pile of leaves, up to her elbows." Waldeen, whom Joe McClain has reproached with being "afraid to do anything new," has been prompted by her memory of a small but "great adventure" to act recklessly. As in the concluding images of many of Mason's stories, optimism is implicit in her momentary embrace of change.

Family ritual also provides the lens through which Mason examines the effect of change in "Drawing Names." The protagonist, Carolyn Sisson, has returned to her parents' home for Christmas Day. The title of the story draws attention to the family's need to improvise a new ritual in response to changing circumstances: members of the family must draw names to determine the recipient of their Christmas gift. Carolyn reflects that she herself "could not afford to buy fifteen presents on her salary as a clerk at J.C. Penney's, and her parents' small farm had not been profitable in years" (95). Through her representation of the social microcosm of a family Christmas, Mason subtly explores the changes that are exerting pressure on a family whose relations have been altered by dispersal, separation, and divorce. The effects of feminism are again presented as one of the major sources of change. This is exemplified by a brief exchange that is typical of Mason's finely attuned use of dialogue to offer a pithy insight into the conjunction of characters' emotions with cultural circumstance. As most of the male members of the family hurry to finish the Christmas dinner so they can watch the television, the grandfather remarks "Use to, the menfolks would eat first, and the children separate. The womenfolks would eat last, in the kitchen." One of his granddaughters comments that "times are different now. . . . We're just as good as the men," to which the husband from whom she is separating remarks, "She gets that from television" (104).[16] Other social changes are lightly alluded to as the family discusses, bemused, the "black Barbie doll" that was given as a Christmas present to a friend of one of Carolyn's nieces. The introduction of change is most marked by the presence of the Northern outsider, Jim Walsh, with whom Carolyn's younger sister, Laura Jean, is "stacking up." Other members of the family respond with circumspection to the educated Jim, as class difference is evinced by his introduction of unfamiliar knowledge into the conversation at the dinner table. This is again evoked by Mason through a poignant moment of dialogue as Jim responds to the father's labored joke about monks with the earnest observation that "The Trappist Monks are a really outstanding group. . . . And they make excellent bread. No preservatives" (103).

These changes are observed by Carolyn as she awaits the arrival of her own boyfriend, Kent Ballard. Carolyn's realization that he is not going to keep his appointment with her family, having gone to see his boat instead, leads to a series of recognitions that enable her to begin to accept some of the changes that she and her family have found painful. As in "Old Things," this story ends with a fantasy that draws together the threads of the narrative in an ameliorative movement, even if it does not offer resolution. The story concludes with Carolyn looking at the box of the bottle of bourbon that Jim has brought as a gift, to be warily received by the family as a confirmation of his unwelcome disruption of their own traditions. The box "showed an old-fashioned scene, children on sleds in the snow," which prompts "Carolyn to think of Kent's boat again. She felt she was in that snowy scene now with Laura Jean and Jim, sailing in Kent's boat into the winter breeze, into falling snow. She thought of how silent it was out on the lake, as though the whiteness of the snow were the absence of sound" (108). While the significance of the silence and whiteness in Carolyn's fantasy remains indeterminate, the presence of Laura Jean and Jim on the boat with her suggests the healing of certain rifts. Throughout the Christmas celebrations, Carolyn has regarded her sister's boyfriend with envious circumspection, until a brief exchange with him has revealed his sensitivity to her own predicament and his commitment to her sister. Prior to the concluding fantasy, Carolyn has "wondered what [Laura Jean and Jim] said to each other when they were alone in St. Louis. She knew they would not be economical with words, like the monks in the story. She longed to be with them, to hear what they would say" (107). Following upon this reflection, the concluding images suggest that Carolyn is reaching an acceptance of what has now become her past, as the fantasy incorporates Kent's boat but not Kent, while she also envisions sailing into an unknown future with people who have embraced departure and change.

In "Offerings" Mason describes Sandra Lee's search for a romanticized rural past, having moved into an isolated country home following the departure of her husband for Louisville, where he works at a K Mart. The story tells of a visit by Sandra's mother and paternal grandmother to Sandra's home. Sandra "presses Grandmother to talk about the past, to tell about the farm Sandra can barely remember," (56) and she tells her visitors that she is collecting "duck expressions" such as "lucky duck," "set your ducks in a row," and "sitting duck" (55–56). Grandmother Stamper is not, however, nostalgic about farm life: after spending five years nursing her dying husband on a "dying farm," she has remarried, has moved into a city apartment, and "has more shoes than places to go." She observes to Sandra: "I declare . . . you have moved plumb out into the wilderness" (54).

Away from the close scrutiny of her grandmother and the dominating masculinity of her husband who, Sandra believes, wants her to spend weekends with him "watching go-go dancers in smoky bars" and whom she expects to return for his hunting rifle, Sandra has taken a defiant pride in neglecting herself and her house. In a flat, controlled tone, which heightens by contrast the abnegation of control that she is describing, Mason notes how "Sandra never dusts," despite her grandmother's warning that if she didn't, "the dust bunnies would . . . multiply and take over," and she "has not mowed in three weeks." However, there are signs of the menace of the wilderness, and of Sandra's defenselessness against it: a missing cat may have been shot and a bird she tried to rescue from another cat "died in her hand" and is on a stump, "untouched since yesterday" (53). More worryingly, perhaps, although it is late summer, Sandra has not made any preparations for winter, letting her woodpile get low and failing to insulate the attic or repair a leak in the basement.

Underlying Sandra's apparent nonchalance about the encroachment of the wilderness is a fear of the invasion of the body, particularly the female body, by pain, illness, and death, when preventative action is not taken. The story opens with Sandra reflecting on the death of her maternal grandmother "of childbed fever at the age of twenty-six." She then recalls how her mother "developed an infection but was afraid to see the doctor," insisting "it would go away." Years later, her mother experienced "inexplicable pains," and she recalls her mother's gruesome account of the operation that followed: "Through blurred eyes, she could see a red expanse below her waist. It resembled the Red Sea parting . . ." (53). Her mother's hysterectomy becomes one of several secrets kept between the women of the family: Sandra's mother has never told her mother-in-law about it, nor, for twenty-five years, about the fact that she smokes, and she now warns Sandra to protect Grandmother Stomper from the knowledge that Sandra's husband has left. The morbidity aroused by these feminine secrets haunts Sandra as she enjoys the temporary womanly community afforded by her relatives' visit: the tomato soup she has prepared resembles "bowls of blood," and she glimpses on the television "a star formed by women, with spread legs, lying on their backs in the water" (58–9).

Through the images of the concluding sequence of the story, Mason subtly draws its themes together and gives them an unexpected twist. As Sandra accompanies her mother outside for her to smoke a secret cigarette, she dispassionately recalls how yesterday her cats ate a mole, starting with its nose, "like a delicacy." Her next memories of the feral nature of the wild are oddly nuanced, however. Threatening savagery is turned into choreographed beauty as Sandra recalls the "menacing yaps" of foxes at night and then how fox cubs playing in the moonlight resembled "dancers in a spotlight." She remembers how "she heard a baby screaming in terror," a cry that she recognized to be that of a wildcat. This sound has become "a thrill she listens for every night," suggesting that Sandra herself is developing an increasingly feral pleasure in wildlife. These images culminate in Sandra's reflection that "she would not mind if the wildcat took her ducks. They are her offering" (59). This open-ended statement gives one pause to wonder whether Sandra desires to pro-pitiate the wilderness without or within her, a wildness which she both fears and desires.

The concluding images extends this ambiguity: "The night is peaceful, and Sandra thinks of the thousands of large golden garden spiders hidden in the field. In the early morning the dew shines on their trampolines, and she can imagine bouncing with an excited spring from web to web, all the way up the hill to the woods" (59). The tranquil beauty evoked by the first image is disturbed by the metamorphosis of Sandra that occurs through the predatory exuberance of her identification with the spiders. Albert Wilhelm has observed that this passage has been inter-preted as "beautifully" and "positively" offering "a metaphor for connections among women (especially mother and daughter) that illustrates their power to sustain each other in times of cri-sis."[17] Wilhelm argues, however, that this reading "overlooks the ominous overtones of this elaborate fairy-tale image. In the spi-derweb conceit, Sandra sees herself moving not toward social involvement but deeper into the lonely woods. Furthermore, her means of getting there is frail and insubstantial. Instead of bounc-ing her to ever greater heights, the flimsy webs would surely break and cling." Wilhelm concludes that "Sandra is more caught in a web than soaring above it."[18] This reading is a per-ceptive response to the ambiguities that pervade the imagery of the story. The "woods" that Sandra perceives as a welcoming retreat from the social relations that have constricted or hurt her do indeed, as in fairy-tales, also connote to the reader a wilder-ness where she may find herself abandoned to both exterior and interior untrammeled nature.

In "Nancy Culpepper" Mason explores her eponymous protagonist's attempts to integrate the past with the present. The story tells of Nancy's return to her parents' home as they are about to move her grandmother into a nursing home. Nancy has moved to Pennsylvania after attending graduate school and marrying Jack Cleveland, "a Yankee," in Massachusetts. Having felt exiled throughout her years in the North, she has now become preoccupied with recovering some family photographs she believes to be hidden in a closet in her grandmother's home. Mason vividly evokes Nancy's sense of culture shock as she was initiated into Northern middle-class culture through her description of Nancy's memories of her wedding. Nancy recalls how, after persuading her parents not to attend the wedding, she felt only alienation and homesickness. This is accentuated by the icons of 1960s counter-culture that mark the occasion, such as "Sgt. Pepper's Lonely Hearts Club Band" playing "instead of organ music" and a chain-smoking minister whom the preachers of her childhood "would have called a heathen." "Dope" and a "wine-and-7Up punch" are served for refreshments, their heady insubstantiality contrasting with what Nancy thinks her parents might be eating for supper: "Possibly fried steak, two kinds of peas, biscuits, blackberry pie" (182). The wedding photographs turn out to be "trick photography," which underscores Nancy's sense of the inauthenticity of the ritual when separated from the traditions that would have conferred significance on it in the culture of her childhood. As Nancy dances with her husband to the Beatles record, she laments: "There aren't any stopping places. . . . Songs used to have stopping places in between" (182). Nancy's return to Kentucky to find her grandmother's photographs becomes a search for a place in which to pause and reflect on the changes that have transformed her life and culture.[19]

On an earlier return to Kentucky, Nancy finds that her acquisition of middle-class tastes has estranged her from the landscape of her childhood. She believes that, divested of the value that labor, familiarity, and memory would confer upon it, the landscape would seem merely a quaint composition. Nancy imagines that Jack "was seeing peaceful landscapes—arrangements of picturesque cows, an old red barn. She had never thought of the place this way before; it reminded her of prints in a dime store" (184). To Nancy, Jack's photographs denaturalize Nature by turning it into Art, as he composes still-life images out of "common" things such as "stumps, puffballs, tree roots, close-ups of cat feet" (186).

Nancy's return to her childhood home to find the photograph of her namesake becomes an attempt to recover her connection to the past. Her earlier discovery of the inscription NANCY CULPEPPER, 1833–1905 on a tombstone in a local cemetery seemed like "time-lapse photography. . . . I was standing there looking into the past and future at the same time. It was weird" (186–7). In her sense of standing on a threshold, at a point of transition between past and future, Nancy epitomizes many of Mason's women characters. At present, Nancy prefers to look to the past to secure her identity, and since discovering the existence of her great-great-aunt, she has started using her maiden name. When she finds a wedding photograph of the woman she believes to be her namesake, Nancy recognizes in her a precursor whose conflicting longings anticipate her own, but who would be able to embrace the future: "This young woman would be glad to dance to 'Lucy in the Sky with Diamonds' on her wedding day, Nancy thinks. The man seems bewildered, as if he did not know what to expect, marrying a woman who has her eyes fixed on something so far away" (195).

Nancy Culpepper reappears in the next story of the collection, "Lying Doggo," where the dying of her husband's dog, Grover, seems to mark "a milestone" in "a marriage that has somehow lasted almost fifteen years" (198). This story extends the themes of "Nancy Culpepper" as it traces Nancy's reflections on the tensions caused in her marriage by the initial class differences between herself and her husband, which are caricatured in Nancy's observation to Jack that "You educated me. I was so out of it when I met you. One day I was listening to Hank Williams and shelling corn for the chickens and the next day I was expected to know what wines went with what" (207).

In each of these stories, Mason's protagonists are adapting to the changes that occur as familiar traditions of rural life in western Kentucky are being replaced by the images and ideology introduced by consumer culture. In the stories Mason shows how the process of adaptation is a gradual one, attained through moments of recognition in which the past is brought to bear on the interpretation of the present. This process is inscribed with a sense of what is being lost and often generates anxiety and fear, but, as Mason shows, individual and cultural identities may be tentatively renewed through it. The characters' assimilation to an "Americanizing" consumer culture is imitated by Mason's style, with its naturalization of references to consumer products. In some of the stories, however, consumer culture retains its

strangeness as Mason uses defamiliarizing techniques to empha-
size the apparently incongruous juxtaposition of the values
embedded in past traditions with the ideology imparted by the
images and artifacts of consumer culture. Linda Adams Barnes
has suggested that Mason's revelation of the incongruity of this
juxtaposition adds an element of the grotesque to her work,
which locates it in a tradition of Southern grotesque descending
from Flannery O'Connor. She argues that although inherent in
O'Connor's use of the grotesque is a faith that assumes "the possibility of grace," a faith that has largely disappeared from the
world evoked by Mason, Mason's stories also imply a moral
vision through the "instructiveness" of her "dramatization" of
the conflict between "traditional Southern life and encroaching
modern life."[20] This effect of grotesqueness that unsettles the
spare surface created by the precise, literal details of dirty realist
writing has also been described as "a kind of surrealism of the
everyday."[21]

One story that emphasizes the strangeness of the everyday is
"Detroit Skyline, 1949." This story is an anomaly in the collection in that it is told by a first-person narrator ("Residents and
Transients" is the only other example of this) and the events of
the story take place in a Northern industrial city in 1949 rather
than in Mason's usual setting of contemporary Kentucky. The
narrator is recalling a journey she made as a nine-year-old girl to
visit relatives in Detroit. Mason's use of a first-person narrator
allows her to create an impression of interiority that contrasts
with most of the stories, where she allusively infers her characters' states of mind through the evocation of their perception of
external details, as recounted by a third-person narrator.[22] Her use

of a child's point of view also enables her to defamiliarize the "reality" to which adults become inured.[23] By setting the story in the post—World War II period, Mason historicizes some of the changes that her other stories represent, particularly as much of her narrator's sense of wonder and disorientation is aroused by the commodities that she is encountering for the first time. The narrative frame of a journey from western Kentucky to Detroit (a reversal of most of the journeys undertaken in Mason's stories) focuses the conflict between rural and urban culture that is to become more complex and pervasive in the contemporary world of Mason's other stories.

Peggy Jo learns from fragments of her aunt's and uncle's conversation that the Detroit in which she has arrived with her mother is darkened by people's fear of "reds" and immobilized by a bus strike caused by "trouble with the unions." Against this backdrop, Peggy Jo is fascinated by such "strange" manifestations of consumer culture as a "toaster, a Mixmaster," an advertisement of "a fabulous life with Fab," and a "Toni doll . . . with a Play Wave, including plastic spin curlers and Toni Creme Rinse" (44). Most fascinating and astonishing of all, she finds, is the television, which begins to permeate her imagination. The cultural collision between North and South evinced by the child's response to these commodities is immediately interpreted by her Detroit relatives as a class difference, the result of being "raised with a bunch of country hicks" (38). The child's sense of the strangeness of the everyday reality of life in Detroit is amplified by her aunt's scrapbooks of newspaper clippings, which "included household hints and cradle notes, but most of the stories were about bizarre occurrences around the world—diseases and kidnappings and disasters." Her aunt explains: "Life is amazing. I keep these to remind me of just how strange everything is" (42). To the adult, in contrast with the child, the defamiliarization of the quotidian only occurs when extremity or anomaly reveals its "bizarreness." Mason's adult characters generally adjust to the intrusion of the unfamiliar in their lives by assimilating it to the familiar, which involves a denial of differences. Mason's mimetic representation of this process through a preponderance of similes and metonymy over metaphor creates the "flattening" effect of her writing. The stories invented by Peggy Jo, however, exemplify a child's desire to find narratives that explain both the differences and the connections between things. These narratives necessarily become metaphoric as layers of "reality," imagined and literal, cultural and "natural," are interpreted through each other. For example, Peggy Jo's familiar world is further unsettled when her mother, who has been taken to hospital, explains to her that she has "lost" a baby. The child forms a narrative to try and understand what has happened: "That night, alone in the pine-and-cedar room, I saw everything clearly, like the sharpened images that floated on the television screen. My mother had said an egg didn't hatch, but I knew better. The reds had stolen the baby. They took things. They were after my aunt's copper-bottomed pans. They stole the butter. They wanted my uncle's job. They were invisible, like the guardian angel, although they might wear disguises. You didn't know who might be a red. You never knew when you might lose a baby that you didn't know you had " (50). Peggy Jo's explanatory narrative is a bricolage of fragments of overheard adults' gossip, other children's lore, and the images she has received from the television, radio, and children's books.

On her return journey to the South, the child is seized by the sense of wonder that Mason's adults have largely lost: "I felt—with a new surge of clarity—the mystery of travel, the vastness of the world, the strangeness of life" (51). Momentarily the child fears that her father and brother will not recognize her and her mother when they return, but she is reassured by seeing that "our little white house was still there" (52). To Mason's adults, however, the concept of "home" is always destabilized by departure and return.

Mason explores this theme further in "Still Life with Watermelon," another story where "reality" is unsettled by elements of the grotesque. Louise Milsap is trying to adjust to the loss of her job and the impulsive departure of her husband to work on a ranch in Texas. Her friend, Peggy, has moved in with her, as her husband has also left "unconscionably." Peggy seeks a pattern to the apparent randomness of contemporary life, in Harlequin romances and "dreams and coincidences," and she persuades Louise to paint watermelons in the hope of selling them to a rich, old eccentric who has taken to collecting paintings of watermelons. Louise has tried to accommodate the events that have dramatically altered her life, but if she has managed to suppress a recognition of their untowardness, a sense of strangeness imbues her surreal paintings of watermelons: "the first one she tried looked like a dark-green basketball floating on an algae-covered pond" (60), and others "appear to be optical illusions—watermelons disappearing like black holes into vacant skies" (67). The incongruity between the watermelons and the backgrounds against which she paints them hovers as an image of her own life.

Louise has refused to accompany her husband on his adventure, preferring the safety of "home," but upon his return she reflects that "Tom is home and she doesn't know what that means" (71). When Herman Priddle is unable to buy her paintings, she realizes that perhaps it is she "who has been off on a crazy adventure" (73). This recognition leads her to connect her own experience to larger social changes: "Something about the conflicting impulses of men and women has gotten twisted around. . . . She had preached the idea of staying home, but it occurs to her now that perhaps the meaning of home grows out of the fear of open spaces. In some people that fear is so intense that it is a disease. . ." (73).

Bill and Imogene Crittendon in "The Ocean" have embraced "open spaces," having sold their farm and bought a camper in which to travel down to Florida. As in "Shiloh" and "Detroit Skyline, 1949," the journey out of the insularity of their home state prompts the characters to make historical and geographical comparisons—albeit of a fragmentary nature—which are rare among Mason's characters. Bill has initiated the journey so that he may see the ocean for the first time since he was serving on a ship on the Pacific in the Second World War. As he travels down to Florida, Bill is disturbed by nightmares in which various parts of his past coexist alarmingly: "He had a nightmare in which his mother and Imogene sat in rocking chairs on either side of him, having a contest to see who could rock the longest. Bill's job was to keep the score, but they kept on rocking" (161).

The "endless rocking" leaves Bill feeling "seasick" and "frightened." Bill's nightmare is permeated by anxiety about his wife's distress at their strange translation from life on the farm to life on the road. This anxiety is reflected in his confusion about both the past and the present as, finally looking out to sea, he imagines "battleships and destroyers" there and cannot "tell if they were coming or going, or whose they were" (164).

An element of the grotesque, which draws attention to the strangeness of the intersection of contemporary culture with rural traditions, is present in three other stories through Mason's representation of women's illnesses.[24] In "The Climber," "The Retreat," and "Third Monday" Mason depicts women whose illnesses draw attention to their confinement in their bodies. This occurs in a culture that isolates them through the "disembodiment" of its media of communication, such as the telephone, television, and information technology. Bodily confinement serves as a figure for the way in which Mason's characters are enclosed within their culture, despite the proliferation of media of communication, and feel unable to actively connect with historical changes. In these stories this confinement is gendered, as men provide images of a freedom that still seems unavailable to the women.

"The Climber" tells of Dolores, who is waiting to keep an appointment with a doctor about what she fears is breast cancer. Dolores's sense that possibilities for her are restricted by her body is contrasted with the images of masculine transcendence that open the story. Dolores is watching an interview with an astronaut on "the Christian channel": "The former astronaut claims that walking on the moon was nothing, compared to walking with Jesus . . ." (109). These images of escape from bodily limitation lead to another, closer to home, as Dolores watches a tree-cutter at work in her yard. The tree-cutter takes risks, Dolores observes, "as though to fall would be incidental" (118). By contrast, Dolores feels immured in her body by her fear about her illness and spends her time talking on the telephone to her friend who has had a catalogue of illnesses. Dolores reflects that "whenever women get together, they talk about diseases. Men never do" (110). This contrast is underscored for the reader by an implied simile: while Dolores lies on the doctor's examination table, the tree "filled with plump green buds" is cut down. Although she is relieved to discover that her symptoms are benign, she, like Louise Milsap in "Still Life With Watermelon," feels bereft of her own sense of adventure. She "somehow felt cheated. She wonders what it would take to make a person want to walk with the Lord, a feeling that would be greater than walking on the moon" (120).

A similarly grotesque conjunction of images occurs in "The Retreat," which tells of a moment of crisis in the marriage of Georgeann and Shelby Pickett, a part-time evangelical preacher. Georgeann's increasing sense of disorientation is manifested in symptoms that could have been caused by the mites of a sick chicken. She expresses her unhappiness at a retreat that she has reluctantly attended with her husband, as she asks: "What do you do if the man you're married to . . . turns out to be the wrong one for you?" When her question falls on deaf ears, Georgeann retreats to the basement, where she starts playing video games. These, she discovers, enable her to project herself into a virtual space beyond the confines of her body and her marriage: "The situation is dangerous and thrilling, but Georgeann feels in control. She isn't running away; she is chasing the aliens" (145). She responds to Shelby's perplexity about her new pastime with the explanation: "You forget everything but who you are . . . Your mind leaves your body" (146). This experience seems purgative, enabling Georgeann to make the decision not to accompany her husband when he moves to another church. The ending is ambiguous, however, suggesting that Georgeann's beheading of the sick chicken may be either a further act of excision or a resumption of her former role of dutiful wife: "When the ax crashes blindly down on its neck, Georgeann feels nothing, only that she has done her duty" (147).

"Third Monday" opens with an image of both women's freedom from former social control of their sexuality and their continued circumscription within the body. Ruby, who has undergone a radical mastectomy, is participating in a celebration that is "an amazing baby shower because Linda is thirty-seven and unmarried" (232). Ruby herself is enjoying an unconventional relationship with Buddy Landon, whom she sees only on the third Monday of each month, as he travels "the flea-market circuit" selling dogs. While Buddy's transience allows Ruby a certain freedom, her cancer seemed to have a grotesque "presence of its own," "interfering" with her actions and choices "like a nosy neighbor." Ruby's adjustment to the loss of both her breast and Buddy, whom she learns is in jail, is evoked through a transfigurative pattern of images. In the concluding scene Mason describes how Ruby meets a man who is visiting the clinic for a "brain test": "The man picks up a magazine and says, 'this is my baby.' He hugs the magazine and rocks it in his arms.

His broad smile curves like the crescent phase of the moon"
(247). Ruby's sense of both loss and optimism is evoked by this
final image. At one level it is a grotesque transformation of the
story's opening image of the celebration of Linda's unborn child
and it also alludes to Ruby's bodily loss. However, the moon has
also been associated with Ruby's sense of freedom as she looked
at it with Buddy and later, recovering, albeit with a sense of loss,
from her operation, noted that "Everything is round and full now,
like the moon" (242).

In "A New-Wave Format" Mason again explores the possibility of transforming the present by revisiting the past. Edwin
Creech, who is in his early forties, has begun a relationship with
the twenty-year-old Sabrina and has started a new job, driving a
bus for "mentally retarded adults." As he becomes aware of the
different values he and Sabrina hold, Edwin begins to reflect on
his life. He realizes that "he still feels like the same person,
unchanged, that he was twenty years ago" (215). Edwin feels
that the historical events of the Sixties, the period of his youth,
did not directly touch him. By contrast, he now feels a new
excitement as he tries to protect the delicate equilibrium of the
passengers on his bus: "Edwin has to stay alert, for anything
could happen. The guys who came back from Vietnam said it
was like this every moment. Edwin was in the army, but he was
never sent to Vietnam, and now he feels that he has bypassed
some critical stage in his life: a knowledge of terror" (217). He
realizes that his immersion in the popular culture of television
and radio has acted as a kind of opiate, dissociating him from the
events in his life that might have produced strong emotions. He
reflects that "he used to think of himself as an adventurer, but

now he realizes that he has gone through his life rather blindly, without much pain or sense of loss" (216). However, as he plays Sixties music to his passengers, "music that now seems full of possibility: the Grateful Dead, the Jefferson Airplane, groups with vision," Edwin listens to it with a new understanding. For Edwin, unlike many of Mason's characters, listening again to the music of his past enables him to create "a bridge from the past to the present, spanning those empty years—his marriages, the turbulence of the times—and connecting his youth solidly with his present" (228). The healing effect of integrating the music of the past with his present circumstances is contrasted with the effect of the "new-wave format," the contemporary music that Sabrina persuades Edwin to play to his passengers on the bus: "The frenetic beat was a perfect expression of their aimlessness and frustration" (228). The "grotesque" confinement of his passengers in the frenetic beat of the present moment is highlighted when one of them has a seizure. Edwin himself, however, feels that he has overcome a "developmental disability" by revisiting the past. Through his newly compassionate perception, it becomes not the passengers on the bus who are grotesque (as they are to Sabrina) but the dislocations between the various moments of his life and the abandonment to a disconnected present that is expressed in the "frantic beat" of the music of the "new-wave format."[25] In its exploration of a character's attempt to integrate the legacy of the 1960s with the present moment in order to reach a new understanding of himself and his culture, this story anticipates the central theme of Mason's next work, *In Country*.

CHAPTER THREE

In Country

Mason's first novel, *In Country* (1985), was generally well-received by reviewers and has generated much critical attention. A commercially successful film adaptation of the book was released in 1989.[1] The novel tells of the double quest of its seventeen-year-old protagonist, Samantha Hughes, to learn about her father, who died in the Vietnam War before she was born, and to heal her uncle Emmett, a Vietnam veteran whom she believes was traumatized by the war. Through her quest Samantha undergoes a rite of passage from adolescence to womanhood. As Joel Conarroe has observed, in "a timely variation on the traditionally male-centred *Bildungsroman,*" Samantha "passes through the phases traditionally associated with . . . rites of passage, progressing from separation to isolation (confronting a heart of darkness) and fictionally to integration."[2]

Mason has acknowledged the influence of her childhood reading on her decision to write a feminine rite-of-passage novel. She has recalled wishing to "write a kind of *Huckleberry Finn* novel about a *girl,*"[3] and she has claimed a "basic identification" with the protagonists of the girl detective books, with their "very innocent dreams of quests for clarity, solving a mystery, and wanting to go somewhere, do something and be somebody."[4] These books, Mason has noted, "use the trappings of the mystery genre . . . to glamorize the trespass into adulthood."[5] If "the ordinary life of the female had three episodes: menstruation, marriage, and motherhood,"[6] the girl sleuth narratives offered their young readers images of adventure and freedom. Moreover, in the pre-second-wave-feminist era of the Nancy Drew books, their eponymous heroine "doesn't have to confront feminist anxieties,"[7] but "she always has it both ways—protected and free. She is an eternal girl, a stage which is a false ideal for women in our time."[8] In her preference for adventure over domesticity and her detective-like quest to solve the mystery of her past, Samantha Hughes bears the imprint of the girl sleuth. But, on the threshold of contemporary womanhood, her quest must lead her out of the mythical timelessness of "protected" innocence into the equivocal freedom of history.

Most of *In Country* takes place in the small town of Hopewell, western Kentucky, in the early 1980s. As seen through "Sam's" eyes, rural Kentucky has been largely subsumed by a "generic American" consumer culture[9] comprised of subdivisions, shopping malls, commodities, fast food chains, television, and rock songs. Some critics have questioned whether Mason's decision to focus such a subject as the effects of the Vietnam War upon "America" through the consciousness of a seventeen-year-old girl whose main source of knowledge is consumer culture is an unnecessarily limiting one. Fred Hobson, for example, wonders whether Mason is fulfilling her "responsibility as a novelist" in creating Sam Hughes, "a point-of-view character to whom all is of nearly equal significance . . . so connected are her points of reference, her mythology, to mass culture, to an artificial rendering of experience."[10] He concludes that *In Country* does offer "a meditation on history" but that "minimalism and history do not mix well" and that "minimalist fiction requires a non-minimalist reader." As, in Hobson's view, Samantha Hughes does not provide the references and knowledge necessary to interpret history, the reader "must draw on knowledge or experience *external to the story*."[11] Joel Conarroe offers a similar argument about the discrepancy between the intended reader and the narrative consciousness of *In Country*. He posits that central to the novel's "Shopping Mall Realism" is the fact that Sam "is no reader" and that the novel is "less resonant" because of this. Despite this, he commends the novel as an "exceptional achievement" in which "every detail, however trivial, is put in for a reason, and patterns of considerable sophistication . . . emerge."[12] As other critics have recognized, however, part of Mason's "achievement" in *In Country* is the way she depicts the development of Sam as a reader, as she negotiates between different cultures, questioning values relating to traditional concepts of family, community, home and gender, and searching for new forms of knowledge.[13] Like the girl sleuth before her, Sam must "attempt to fit together pieces of the puzzle, to see the pattern, to comprehend the mystery,[14] and, through reading the signs of her culture, "to write her own story."[15] Steeped as Sam is in popular cultural references, the concept that her quest brings under greatest scrutiny is that of history. As she tries to learn about her father by informing herself about the Vietnam War, she begins to question the nature of history and truth and the ways in which these can be known. Her quest for information about the war leads her to gather fragments of oral testimony from her uncle, Emmett, and Hopewell's other Vietnam veterans. Mason's portrayal of the veterans creates the second thematic focus of the novel, an examination of the effects of the war on American culture and people. She extends this focus to consider the reverberations of other social and cultural changes introduced in the 1960s through the 1980s. The novel suggests that foremost among the legacies of the Sixties is the transformation of traditional gender roles, and an examination of the way in which these roles are constructed provides its main subtext.

Like many of the stories in *Shiloh, In Country* is inscribed with a sense of loss, as the narrative balances the personal and cultural gains that are the product of the choices offered by consumer culture against the losses that are the perceived cost of these gains. Mason's representation of the effects of the Vietnam War on the inhabitants of a small town in western Kentucky "testifies to the end of the cultural and historical isolation of the South,"[16] but it also reveals a people in mourning. Above all, they are mourning the "country boys" who died in the war, the official justifications of whose death they may find hard to accept. More generally, they are mourning a loss of belief in authority, due in part to the widespread questioning of the narratives that were used to legitimate American involvement in the war. Sam Hughes undertakes her search for knowledge about the war partly to bring to a close the process of mourning for a father whom she has never known. Sam's quest, the novel suggests, is part of a larger cultural process of mourning that has not, in the mid 1980s, been brought to closure.

The novel opens in the present tense with Samantha Hughes, Emmett, and her paternal grandmother, Mamaw, driving from Kentucky to the Vietnam Veterans Memorial in Washington. Their journey is contextualized by the retrospective second section, which narrates Samantha's quest, which has culminated in the visit to the memorial. This section begins: "It was the summer of the Michael Jackson *Victory* tour and the Bruce Springsteen *Born in the U.S.A.* tour, neither of which Sam got to go to."[17] This sentence immediately indicates how Sam's consciousness has been shaped by the events and personalities of popular culture. But the beginning of the summer of 1984 was also marked by the speech the minister had made at her high school graduation ceremony "about keeping the country strong, stressing sacrifice" (23). As Sam faces the choice of what to do next, she also begins to reflect on the past, and particularly the Vietnam War. An adolescent wondering about her identity, she looks to a photograph of her father, Dwayne Hughes, aged nineteen, for confirmation of who she is, but when she compares this with her own face in the mirror, "She couldn't see any resemblance to him" (58). Her desire to find out more about her father motivates her to start out on the quest that will teach her much about her culture, as well as her own identity.

At the outset of the narrative, Sam spends most of her time working in the Burger Boy, jogging, and with her boyfriend, Lonnie Malone, or friend Dawn. Both Sam and Dawn are proud of the independence that their roles in their nontraditional families have conferred upon them. Since Dawn's mother died, she has looked after her father and brothers, and Sam lives with her veteran uncle Emmett, since her mother's remarriage and departure to Lexington. Despite their caring attitudes toward their relatives, Sam and Dawn cultivate an image of rebelliousness,[18] which is put to the test when Dawn discovers she is pregnant and Sam advocates abortion. The prospect of Dawn having either a baby or an abortion haunts both girls. Sam feels a visceral revulsion at the thought of Dawn's baby and wakes in horror after a dream in which she and the Vietnam veteran Tom Hudson "had a baby. In the evening, the baby had to be pureed in a food processor and kept in the freezer. It was the color of candied sweet potatoes. In the morning, when it thawed out, it was a baby again" (83). Dawn tells Sam of how, after buying a chicken, she "pulled out those parts inside, all wrapped in paper" and "I had the sickening thought that the chicken was giving birth to a creature, but it was all in parts, so they had to be stuffed in a little bag" (176). Sam is also nauseated by what seems to be the superannuated fecundity of her thirty-seven-year-old mother, whose baby, a "growth" upon Irene, "was more like a vegetable than a human—with its odd sick smell and pulsation, like a watermelon growing fast in the night" (162). In *The Girl Sleuth* Mason recounts how she has been tormented since adolescence by "recurring food dreams" in which she "has to choose from a thousand beautiful foods," which she interprets as expressing her guilt at her complicity with her country's ideology of consumption.[19] A later allusion in *The Girl Sleuth* to the "stereotype of passive female consumerism"[20] casts some light on Sam's and Dawn's position as they stand on the threshold of womanhood.[21]

As adolescents, Sam and Dawn are targets of a consumer culture that both exploits women through its images of them as commodities and denies women's lived experience of their bodies. Sam fears that the consequence for Dawn of her baby will be entrapment in marriage and motherhood, and both girls fantasize about being freed from this destiny through the images of femininity that consumer culture offers them. Dawn wishes that they "could go hang out at one of those bars in Paducah where those

traveling businessmen go. We could wear our sexiest outfits and
they'd think we were a lot older. Maybe they'd buy us something
to eat and give us some money" (43). They fantasize about making a video in which they will "wear black leather pants and sun-
glasses with bright pink rims," (104) and Sam tries to persuade
Dawn to go with her to work at Disney World. In these fantasies
they see the commodification of themselves as a preferable alternative to the fate of motherhood, which seems to be their bodily
destiny. Dawn, however, resigns herself to the prospect of marriage and motherhood with her boyfriend, Ken. Her acceptance
of conventional femininity is signified to Sam by her bedroom,
with its "delicate gold-and-blue flowered wallpaper and a skirt
on her dressing table" (39). Sam, however, rebels against
women's confinement in such domestic spaces, turning instead
to the freedom represented by the road. Even here, however,
what she perceives as freedom is compromised for women. As
she jogs through a subdivision, she reflects that "when she ran,
she felt free, as if she could do anything," and yet frequently on
her runs, she has been harassed by loitering men (75).

None of the women Sam knows offers her a desirable role
model. Even Anita Stevens, whom Sam admires for her beauty
and her capacity to make Emmett laugh and who is independ-
ently single, appears to Sam "as though she were sitting in a
perfectly arranged setting, waiting for something to happen, like
a stage set just before the curtain goes up" (62). Nor is Sam yet
ready to listen to her mother, who tries to impress upon her that
some changes have taken place for women, who "can do anything now . . . If they go to college" (232). Sam's general sense
of a lack of connection with "history" extends to her apparent

indifference to these changes. Ambivalent toward femininity, as her name suggests, Sam becomes disenchanted by what she sees as the choices for women offered by either traditional or consumer culture. She turns instead to the narratives of masculinity offered by representations of the Vietnam War.

Sam's initial source of information about the war is Emmett, whose condition also fuels her investigations as she tries to find a cure for him. Emmett suffers from symptoms such as acne, which Sam fears were caused by Agent Orange, the herbicide the Americans used to destroy the forests that gave cover to the Vietcong. She recalls how when she was a child, she and Emmett compiled a stamp collection, but "their stamp album was old and the countries were wrong—old colonial countries like Ceylon and the Belgian Congo. Vietnam was Indochine" (51). The stamp album is reminiscent of the map on the wall of Michael Herr's apartment in Saigon, as he describes it at the beginning of the novel *Dispatches*. This map "wasn't real any more," its "buckled" paper "laying a kind of veil over the countries it depicted. Vietnam was divided into its older territories of Tonkin, Annam and Cochin China, and to the west past Laos and Cambodge sat Siam, a kingdom. . . . It was late '67 now, even the most detailed maps didn't reveal much any more; reading them was like trying to read the faces of the Vietnamese, and that was like trying to read the wind."[22] Herr's map, with its lack of correspondence to the Vietnam of 1967, becomes a metaphor for his sense of the impossibility of mapping, and of knowing, the Vietnamese landscape and people. Through the novel Herr nonetheless attempts to create a map of the war, in order to try and reconcile himself retrospectively with his experiences in

Vietnam. In *In Country* Sam Hughes searches for a "map" that will enable her to read what happened to her father in Vietnam, and by knowing this, to accommodate the otherness that the Vietnamese landscape and people represent to her.

From the "war stories" Emmett told her as they made the stamp collection, "Sam had a picture of Vietnam in her mind . . . a pleasant countryside, something like Florida, with beaches and palm trees and watery fields of rice and green mountains" (51). But when Irene stopped Emmett from telling Sam the stories, television became her source of information about Vietnam. Her next memory was of footage of "the fall of Saigon, in 1975 . . . The landscape was believable . . . For the first time, Vietnam was an actual place" (51). Sam's attempt to find out the "truth" about the war becomes, in part, an attempt to imagine the Vietnamese landscape, but she becomes increasingly frustrated by the inauthenticity of television's representations. For example, she recalls watching "a made-for-TV movie" about the war, when "she had been surprised to see soldiers marching through a field of corn. . . . It surprised her that corn grew in Vietnam. She did not know if it was there because Americans had planted it—or had given the Vietnamese the seed and shown them how to plant it—or if in fact corn was ever in Vietnam, since the movie was filmed in Mexico. They certainly had corn in Mexico because corn was an Indian plant. Maize. The woman in the Mazola commercial. It bothered her to find out the truth. Did corn actually grow in Vietnam?" (69–70). Television, she concludes, cannot offer her the "truth" or authenticity she seeks. Emmett appears to share this sentiment, observing, "Johnny Carson has Joan Rivers substituting . . . And it's a rerun. Nothing's authentic anymore" (19).

Nonetheless, television helps to structure Sam's and Emmett's daily lives. M*A*S*H, a sitcom set in Korea, but which "provides an indirect commentary on the Vietnam War,"[23] is particularly significant to them. The repetition of the series reassures them with its familiarity, and the rituals they improvise around their viewing give them a sense of pleasures and knowledge shared with the program's other viewers. In addition, it informs their mourning for the losses they have sustained in the Vietnam War. Sam reflects how "years ago, when Colonel Blake was killed," she "was so shocked she went around stunned for days. She was only a child then, and his death on the program was more real to her than the death of her own father. Even on the repeats, it was unsettling. Each time she saw that episode, it grew clearer that her father had been killed in a war" (25). Although the events portrayed by the series and its repetition cannot bring the process of mourning to closure for Sam, they do contribute to her recognition of the reality of her father's death. Sam is also a critical television viewer, having some awareness of how it has shaped her interpretations of "reality." She believes that if Emmett were to be able to talk about Vietnam, it might cure him of symptoms that could be an effect of repressed memories, but she is also aware that this theory (a popularized version of the psychoanalytic "talking cure"), as demonstrated on M*A*S*H, is probably "too simple."

As television does not seem to be able to tell her the "truth" about Vietnam, Sam turns instead to Hopewell's war veterans.

She is aware that since Emmett returned to Hopewell, he has been regarded as an outsider, and she recalls how, in the 1970s, he and his hippie friends "created a sensation" (23), particularly when they "flew a Vietcong flag from the courthouse tower." "The funny part" of this episode, Emmett points out, "was that nobody had even recognized that it was a Vietcong flag" (24). Since then Emmett has spent his time "doing odd jobs," and he is currently occupied with repairing the basement of their damp and junk-filled house. Mason offers a wryly humorous image of Emmett's psyche as he explains: "My basement's flooded and my foundation's weak. . . . And my house might fall down. . . ." (110). Emmett has constantly been the subject of local rumors, such as that he and Irene were hiding Patty Hearst (24), that he "was the leading dope dealer in town," that he "slept with his niece," and that he "had killed babies in Vietnam" (31).

Critics have applauded Mason's informed and sympathetic representation of the experiences of Vietnam veterans on their return to "the World."[24] Mason's portrayal of the veterans is also attuned to the social significance of popular representations of the veteran, who, as Thomas Myers has observed, has been a figure of "multiple revisions." In his changing role as "scapegoat, monster, victim, avenger," Myers argues, "the veteran is the reflecting surface of our deepest cultural hopes and fears, the most reliable register of life in postmodern America."[25] Mason's portrayal of Sam's quest to "heal" Emmett is a powerful articulation of a particular cultural moment, when the attempt to heal the scars left on the collective psyche by the war has become a national concern.[26] As Mason has remarked, "In the 1980s Vietnam emerged in our culture as a legitimate and compelling topic for discussion, rather than something to be hidden in shame."[27]

Sam's desire to find the "truth" of the war in personal testimony locates her in a cultural moment that values the need to "bring it all back home," and confront what has been hidden, in order to bring the process of mourning to closure.[28] Whereas Emmett will no longer speak of the war, his veteran friends provide Sam with various oral testimonies. Pete, who brought back "ears of the enemy for souvenirs" (123) and who "had a map of Vietnam in the den" until his wife tore it down (50), tells Sam that he feels nostalgic for the war: "It was just the intensity of it, what you went through together. That meant something. . . . There was a dividing line. Life and death" (134). The other veterans echo Pete's view that they have shared an experience that has transformed them, making them different from other people.[29] Tom tells Sam that his ex-girlfriend "wanted everything normal, a family and a ranch house with a two-car garage. She wouldn't have been able to fit in my story" (121). He also confides that "Sometimes I feel homesick for those memories. . . . it's funny how special it was, in a way, like nobody else could ever know what you went through except guys who have been there" (78). Jim, bewailing the poor attendance at the veterans' dance, says: "I thought when you went through something like war together it meant something" (123).

These reminiscences convey to Sam that the veterans share a sense of community, albeit a community of outsiders, formed through sharing the experience of surviving on the borderline between "life and death." She passionately desires to belong to this community, believing that it will define her own identity for her. Attending the veterans' dance, the central communal event in the narrative, she asks: "Don't I belong here? . . . My daddy was in the war" (109). Much as she wants to belong to the community of veterans, Sam is repeatedly told that she will not be able to understand what happened there, and should not try to. Part of the reason for Sam's exclusion from the community of veterans, and the knowledge they share, is her historical inheritance as a woman. Emmett reminds Sam that "women weren't over there. . . . So they can't really understand" (107). The asymmetry of men's and women's relation to war is underlined by Anita Stevens, who tells Sam her "Vietnam story" at the veterans' dance. Anita recounts how, in 1969, some young soldiers got on the bus on which she was traveling. One of them entered into conversation with her and told her that all the soldiers were leaving for Vietnam the following day. Anita concludes: "for years I thought—that was *my* Vietnam experience. . . . It was *real* and I was right there" (116).

Sam aspires to attain her "real" "Vietnam experience" through identification with the experiences of the veterans. In *Dispatches* Michael Herr has evoked how for the Americans in Vietnam, the intensity of their experience seemed to translate bodily identity into pure energy. He describes how this energy was "American and essentially adolescent" and was powered by American myth and technology.[30] Sam Hughes's search for the heightened sense of reality that she believes the veterans experienced in Vietnam leads her to try and tap into the energy of American culture. A powerful source of such energy to her is rock music, which also provides a connection between the period of the war and the present. As she and Emmett listen to a Beatles song on the radio, Emmett reminisces: "When you're in country, there's so little real connection to the World, but those songs—that was as close as we came to a real connection," and Sam reflects that "sometimes the music was full of energy and hope and the words were just the opposite." (111) The "energy" of the war merges with "the energy of the sixties" for Sam: hearing "a previously unreleased cut from 1964" of a Beatles song on the radio, "like voices from the grave," (51) she "felt the energy of the sixties, like desire building and exploding" (52). Just as the music of the Sixties evokes the mood of the period to her, so the music of the eighties captures the essence of the present. Bruce Springsteen's songs in particular at once articulate her awakening adolescent desire and speak of people's experience of the constraints of small-town, working-class culture, from which Sam wishes to escape. The lines of the title song from Springsteen's 1984 album, *Born in the U.S.A.,* which Mason uses as her epigraph, reverberate through the novel with their depiction of a Vietnam veteran who has not been able to adjust to society since his return from the war: "I'm ten years burning down the road / Nowhere to run ain't got nowhere to go." After she has spent the night with Tom Hudson, the veteran who has become the object of her desire, Sam turns on the radio hoping to hear Springsteen and reflects that "there was a secret knowledge in his songs, as though he knew exactly what she was feeling" (138). Springsteen's songs seem to express to Sam how sexual knowledge fuses with knowledge of the experience of the Vietnam War in her fantasies about Tom.[31]

Yet in Tom Hudson, Sam also sees the discrepancy between

the fantasy of energy and intensity she attributes to the veterans' experience in the war and their condition upon their return. As she watches Springsteen perform *Dancing in the Dark* on television, "she kept thinking about what it would be like to dance with Tom. . . . But he could never move with Bruce Springsteen's exuberant energy" (97). Tom's impotence—a condition that Sam suspects Emmett shares—provides one of the novel's central metaphors of the wounded masculinity that the veterans represent. The effect of the Vietnam War upon the veterans becomes the focus of Mason's continuing sympathetic concern with the ways in which "masculinity" has been challenged by various cultural shifts since the 1960s.[32]

In the novel she also examines, however, the constructions of masculinity with which the Vietnam War, like previous wars, called upon men to conform. Sam becomes increasingly disillusioned with her boyfriend, Lonnie Malone, partly because she fears their relationship will lead to her confinement in marriage, motherhood, and Hopewell, but also because he subscribes to a notion of masculinity that, she realizes, has informed an unquestioning endorsement of war. Her skepticism grows as Lonnie recounts how he has participated in the male bonding ritual of a stag night in McCracken County. When Lonnie's father tells her that "My daddy and his daddy both fought, and I felt like I missed out on something important," Sam replies "Is that why we have wars—so guys won't miss out?" (86–7) The novel's main critique of coercive notions of masculinity is made through Emmett, who, on his return from the war, wore "his Army jacket and black boots, with a purple headband running through his wild hair" (23), and currently refuses to take paid work. Recently

Emmett has decided to wear "a long, thin, Indian-print skirt with elephants and peacocks on it" (26) because, as Sam explains, "Klinger wears dresses on M*A*S*H." Emmett's gestures represent the potential for transforming a masculinity that has been damaged by being forced to its extremity in the war. This transformative potential of transgressing conventional models of gender is implied by the image through which Mason evokes Sam's perception of him: "Emmett looked stately in his skirt—tall and broad, like a middle-aged woman who had had several children" (32). But if popular culture offers a space in which play with the conventional signifiers of gender can take place, as Sam's frequent allusions to Boy George, for example, suggest, this has had little effect on the codes of "gender-appropriate behavior" that still prevail in Hopewell.[33]

Emmett's rebellion against appropriately "masculine" behavior is accompanied by a metaphysical quest for a symbolic object through which he can escape from the personal history that American society has bestowed upon him. This is signified by his search for the egret, a bird that, he explains, is indigenous to both the United States and Vietnam. He tells Sam that seeing the egret in the rice paddies "was a good memory. . . . That beautiful bird just going about its business with all that crazy stuff going on around it" (36). Emmett tries to use this one "beautiful" memory as "a Zen exercise for controlling the mind": "If he concentrated on something fascinating and thrilling, like birds soaring, the pain of his memories wouldn't come through. His mind would be full of birds. Just birds and no memories. Flight" (139). As the novel progresses, allusions to birds and flight become increasingly associated with Emmett's and Sam's search for

healing of the scars of grieving. For example, the affection for
Anita Stevens that Emmett is unable to let develop is suggested
by his remark to her that she looks "like a flamingo" (99). Later,
when Emmett has been traumatized by Sam's disappearance to
Cawood's Pond, it is Sam, in her constant attempt to attune herself to Emmett's mode of perception, who notices a Kentucky
cardinal fly past, "a brilliant surprise, a flash of red, like a train
signal" (219). Sam's and Emmett's quests for symbols through
which they can transcend the past and heal themselves is paralleled by the reader's response to the text. Mason's use of such literary devices as the investment of repeated images with
increasing symbolic significance creates textual patterns whose
unity and coherence provides the reader with a means of interpretation that exceeds that offered by the signs of consumer culture available to the characters.

Emmett's quest for the symbolic egret becomes a model to
Sam for her own search for something that will both transcend
and give meaning to her own culture. Mason evokes this search
with typical humor, whilst also lightly underlining how the
metaphors available to Sam are derived precisely from that culture, as Sam uses an aerobics lesson to conceptualize her quest:
"That is what the new feeling [of being on the road] is like: you
know something as well as you can and then you squeeze one
layer deeper and something more is there" (7). But her pursuit of
knowledge about her father reveals a life that suggests entrapment in rural Kentucky culture rather than ways of transcending
it. Unsatisfied with the representations of Vietnam that she has
encountered on television and in her conversations with
Hopewell's veterans, Sam turns to her father's letters home from

the war. Her search for truth in the word of her father reveals that she has not yet completely relinquished the hope that meaning, and her own identity, can be guaranteed by traditional paternal authority.[34] However, since the minister's speech about her "country" at the graduation, Sam has become increasingly skeptical about authority's versions of "the truth." By the time she finds her father's letters, she has become a discerning reader of the way in which institutional discourses have been used to legitimate the war. She is disappointed by her father's recourse to such rhetoric through phrases such as: "I'm proud to serve my country," (180) "be thankful you're an American. Everybody's as happy as me," (181) and "I pray daily for the little babe" (181). Her father's failure to provide "the truth" is most painful when she reads "here's my favorite name: Samuel. It's from the Bible. If it's a girl, name it Samantha. . . . I think it's a name in Chronicles. I've been reading the Bible every night" (182). Trying to verify her father's words, Sam finds that "there was no Samantha in either the first or the second book of Chronicles" (183). Her father's letters, she feels, have offered her neither the "truth" about the war nor authentication of her identity.

Persisting in her quest for her father, Sam goes to visit her paternal grandparents on their farm outside Hopewell. Sam has not visited her grandparents for almost two years, and she reflects that "her roots were here, and she had been here often enough for the place to be familiar, but not enough to really know it" (199). The gap between her father's world and her own, which has been created by recent historical and cultural shifts, is summed up by Sam's reflection earlier in the narrative, when she tells her father's photograph: "You missed Watergate. . . . It was a TV series one summer" (67). As she surveys her grandparents' farm, "trying to see what her father would have known," she is oppressed by what she perceives as the small world of Dwayne Hughes, the "country boy": "Everything he knew was small and predictable: Jesus bugs, blue mold, hound dogs, fence posts. He didn't know about the new consolidated county high school, rock video, M*A*S*H*. He didn't know her" (200). Clutching Dwayne Hughes's diaries, she flees to the shopping mall in Paducah, where she can read the diaries and escape from the dinginess and provincialism of the farm.

If Sam is disappointed by the evasion of "the truth" in her father's letters, she is appalled by his expression of his experience in his diaries. Admissions that Irene "seems too far away to be real" (202) and that the baby she is carrying is an "unreal thought" (204) are mingled with references to the death of a comrade and Dwayne killing a "gook." The landscape he evokes is hot, putrid, and moribund, scattered with corpses that have "a special stink" (203). As Sam reads the diaries, the Vietnamese landscape fuses with that of Dwayne's childhood, her grandparents' farm, with its "decayed smell," dirt and damp: "Sam couldn't get the sensations out of her head: the mangy dog, the ugly baby, the touch-me-nots, the blooming weeds, the rusty bucket, her dumb aunt Donna. . . . And the diary disgusted her, with the rotting corpse, her father's shriveled feet, his dead buddy, those sickly-sweet banana leaves. . . . Now everything seemed so real it enveloped her, like something rotten she had fallen into" (206). These are exactly the landscapes that have been purged by the aseptic and simulated world of consumer culture, as is exemplified by the shopping mall where Sam is reading the diaries.

Repelled as she is by her discovery of what she believes is the "reality" of her father's experience in the Vietnam War, Sam needs to understand how Dwayne could have killed somebody. She attempts to do this by staying the night at Cawood's Pond, a "snake-infested swamp" (34) that is "the last place in western Kentucky where a person could really face the wild" (208). Throughout the narrative Sam has attempted to learn about the Vietnam War both by questioning representations of it and by trying to identify with the veterans' experiences, a process she continues at Cawood's Pond. Mason's description of Sam "in country," "humping the boonies" at Cawood's Pond, draws attention to the way in which her understanding of the Vietnam War will always be limited by her own cultural position, not least by the representations through which her knowledge has been mediated: "It hit her suddenly that this nature preserve in a protected corner of Kentucky wasn't like Vietnam at all. The night sky in Vietnam was a light show, Emmett had said once. . . . She tried to remember the descriptions she had read. It was like fireworks. And the soundtrack was different from bugs and frogs: the *whoosh-beat* of choppers, the scream of jets, the thunderboom of artillery rounds, the mortar rounds, random bullets and bombs and explosions. The rock-and-roll sounds of war" (214).

The scene at Cawood's Pond is a crucial one in which significant thematic and symbolic threads converge, producing revelations for both of the protagonists, which precipitate the novel's denouement. Up to this point, Sam has been profoundly disturbed by what she has regarded as the cultural destinies produced by biological difference: childbirth and motherhood for women, or war for men. She has also rebelled against the cultural connection between these two "destinies," reflecting, after read-ing her father's diaries, that "If men went to war for women, and for unborn generations, then she was going to find out what they went through. Sam didn't think the women or the unborn babies had any say in it. If it were up to women, there wouldn't be any war." A shift in her thinking at this point is indicated by the fact that she qualifies this, though: "No, that was a naive thought. When women got power, they were just like men" (208). Less rationally, her revulsion at these interconnected "destinies" has expressed itself through the images that have haunted her of unwanted or untimely babies in her own culture and dead babies in Vietnam. Katherine Kinney has observed in her discussion of the novel's exploration of the construction of gender: "The com-mon ground between childbearing and war becomes the terrible mutability of the human body, which can be destroyed and reconstituted in endless cycles of birth and death."[35] For exam-ple, thinking that Irene's baby "was like a growth that had come loose . . . like a scab or a wart" led Sam to recall that "in Viet-nam, mothers had carried their dead babies around with them until they began to rot" (164).

A similar train of thought troubles Sam at Cawood's Pond although, significantly, her revulsion is transferred here from babies to abortion. Musing that the Ancient Mariner with the albatross round his neck must have been like "a pregnant woman thrusting her condition on everyone" leads Sam to conclude that women "wouldn't collect teeth and ears for souvenirs," an opin-ion she quickly revises: "Then chills rushed over her. Soldiers murdered babies. But women did too. They ripped their unborn babies out of themselves and flushed them away, squirming and bloody" (215). During this scene, however, Sam moves toward further recognition of her entrenchment in her position as a woman. After having survived a night in "the wilderness," she imagines that "she was in her father's place, in a fox-hole in the jungle," (217) and that she has attained heightened perception, "a new way of seeing" (218). But the reality of the difference between her father's position in Vietnam and her own at Cawood's Pond is underlined when Sam hears someone approaching, whom she fears is a rapist.

The "rapist" turns out to be Emmett, who has come to look for her. Emmett's worry about Sam's disappearance unleashes his grief, which Sam still relies upon television to interpret: "She thought he was going to come out with some suppressed memories of events as dramatic as that one that caused Hawkeye to crack up in the final episode of M*A*S*H" (222). Emmett does indeed tell her a traumatic memory, of how he lay buried for hours under the dead bodies of his comrades. When Sam comments "I saw something like that in a movie on TV," he corrects her: "This was completely different. It really happened" (223). Overcome by a "monstrous and fantastic" sorrow, Emmett explains that he is "damaged. It's like something in the center of my heart is gone and I can't get it back," and that "I work on staying together, one day at a time" (225). Against Sam's belief in catharsis through the confrontation of repressed memories, but consonant with her search for transcendence of her confinement in her culture, Emmett explains: "If you can think about something like birds, you can get outside of yourself, and it doesn't hurt as much. . . . That's the whole challenge for the human race" (226). Further, he observes: "You can't learn from the past. The main thing you learn from history is that you can't learn from history. That's what history *is*" (226). The challenge that Sam, and the narrative as a whole, make to this view, is epitomized by the images that conclude the scene at Cawood's Pond. At the same time, these images suggest Sam's need, as she mourns, to "get outside of " herself. The transformation of Sam's way of seeing through the information she has gained and the questions she has asked about Vietnam is suggested by the image Mason uses to evoke her watching Emmett as she follows him out of the swamp: "He entered a path into the woods and walked faster. Poison ivy curled around his shoes. From the back he looked like an old peasant woman hugging a baby. Sam watched as he disappeared into the woods. He seemed to float away, above the poison ivy, like a pond skimmer, beautiful in his flight" (226). Through this transfiguring image of Emmett, Sam recognizes the specificity of both Vietnam and motherhood. The beginnings of her acceptance of her relation to both of these is configured by the translation of the allusions to both the "peasant woman" and the "baby" into a symbol of beauty that transcends the confinement of the human body in gender and mortality. Mason evokes Sam's movement toward accommodation to the difference of both the Vietnamese and the female body and an assuagement of the guilt she feels for her country's activities in the war in Vietnam.

The immediate effect of this scene, however, is that an apparent reversal of Sam's and Emmett's former roles takes place. Sam feels that she and Emmett have "changed places" and that "she had post-Vietnam stress syndrome" (229). By contrast, the catharsis that Sam had hoped would happen if Emmett were to talk about his memories does indeed seem to have occurred. Emmett recovers his volition and assumes agency, initiating the trip to the Vietnam Veterans Memorial, persuading Dwayne Hughes's mother to come on the trip, and arranging to take over Sam's job at the Burger Boy so he can pay back his debt to the Vietnam Veterans Association.

Emmett's initiation of the journey to the Vietnam Veterans Memorial helps Sam move further in the process of mourning. Since reading her father's diaries, Sam has felt "spacey," and in addition to her identification with the American soldiers in Vietnam, she now feels unprotected against the seeming randomness of her own culture: "So many videos were full of disasters, with everything flying apart, shifting, changing in the blink of an eye. The random images on the screen were swirling, beyond anyone's control; everything was falling, like their fragile house" (230). Television fails to be its usual solace to her, and she feels that Hopewell and its environs do not "pertain" to her. The journey to the memorial, further out of Kentucky than she has ever been, enables her to enter a transitional space in her rite of passage. Part of her quest has been to identify the determinants of her identity in her own culture and to map this through the experiences of American soldiers in Vietnam, but on the road she feels temporarily freed of the coordinates that determine her place. She regrets their possession of a map, observing: "You can't get lost in the United States. . . . I wish I could, though. I wish I'd wake up and not know where I was" (6). On the road she feels she can connect, untrammeled by bodily or cultural constraints, with the energy of "America": "Everything in America is going on here, on the road. Sam likes the feeling of strangeness. They are at a cross-roads: the interstate with traffic headed east and west, and the state road with north-south traffic. She's in limbo, stationed right in the center of this enormous amount of energy" (17). Here, as "everything seems more real than it has ever been," (7) she finds the kind of heightening of sensual perception that she has been seeking. This is intensified by her jogging, which enables her to feel bodily power rather than limitation, and listening to rock music, through which her own adolescent desire fuses with the energy of American popular culture.

Other spaces Sam encounters on the road contribute to her sense of freedom from the constraints she has experienced in Hopewell. A hotel room enables her to feel both anonymity and connectedness to others through "history": "The room is so clean, with no evidence of belonging to anybody, but it has a secret history of thousands of people, their vibrations and essences soaked in the walls and rug" (12). Shopping malls, with their generic stores and products, continue to offer her an escape from regional and domestic cultures. Despite the homogeneity of these stores, Sam is able to use their products to express her own individuality, thus contesting the conformity that consumerism is designed to secure (its marketing of "individualism" through "style" notwithstanding.) For example, after her night with Tom Hudson, Sam had visited the K Mart and bought "a bright red ceramic cat with a big grin on its face and a slit in its back for coins," which reminded her of Moon Pie, her and Emmett's cat (132). She felt that the cat would make a fitting gift for her mother, being "kooky and personal, very expressive," although the cashier remarked that "everybody's buying these cats to set by their fireplaces."[36] After smoking a joint, Sam decorated the cat with her mother's beads and sequins, making it look like "a punk maharajah" (140). On the journey to the memorial, one of the first gestures of reconciliation with herself and others that Sam is to make takes place when she presents Irene with the cat. Irene's unexpected tears of joy, coming shortly after her caution to Sam that "you don't understand how it was back then," (235) indicate her "recognition" and acceptance of both her daughter's similarity to herself and her individuality. In the mall in Maryland, Sam buys a copy of *Born in the U.S.A.,* whose cover depicts Springsteen "facing the flag, as though studying it, trying to figure out its meaning. It is such a big flag the stars don't even show in the picture—just red-and-white stripes" (236). It is with this image of Springsteen as a questioning reader of the cultural icons of "America" that Sam approaches the Vietnam Veterans Memorial.[37]

This memorial, for the creation of which Vietnam veterans campaigned, was dedicated in 1982, and, like *In Country* three years later, it testifies to the desire for national healing of the wounds created by the war. Since Maya Lin created the design for the memorial, the conflicting messages about the war and its place in American "history" that it seems to convey have been the subject of wide controversy. Maya Lin herself is quoted as saying that she intended "to bring out in people the realization of loss and a cathartic healing process," but elsewhere she has observed that "I thought about what death is, what a loss is . . . a sharp pain that lessens with time, but can never quite heal over. A scar." [38] These apparently contradictory views about the possibility of bringing the process of mourning to closure are articulated by the conflicting iconography of the memorial. The memorial is located in the Washington Mall's Constitution Gardens, an area dedicated to commemoration. It comprises two walls of polished black granite, which form a wide "V," the tips of which point to the Washington Monument and Lincoln Memorial. When seen from the air, the symbolic effect of the area overall is to create an impression of a cohesive American history and of a collective American identity through that history.[39] But this perspective is lost as one descends toward the apex of the "V," alongside the more than fifty-eight thousand names inscribed into the panels that form the "wings" of the wall. The names are inscribed in chronological order of loss: they start at the center "with the first death of a soldier in 1959"[40] and move toward the east tip, resuming at the west tip and returning to the center, ending with the last name in 1975.

As Sam, Emmett, and Mamaw draw near the memorial in the Washington Mall, Sam "feels sick with apprehension" at what the memorial will signify and how this will affect her grief. Despite her desire to find something that will transcend her culture, she will not accept the consolation of religious faith, telling herself there is "nobody here but us chickens" (237). Nor is she prepared to accept official justifications of the losses in the war. As she observes how "the Washington Monument rises up out of the earth, proud and tall," she quickly recalls "Tom's bitter comment about it—a big white prick"(238). When they arrive at the memorial, Sam is struck by its conflicting iconography, which mirrors the confusion that, in her own grief, she feels about its symbolic significance. On the one hand, the memorial does not glorify the war or the losses that occurred in its name. It confronts her with the mortality of the lost soldiers, appearing as "a black gash in a hillside" and "like a giant grave, fifty-eight thousand bodies rotting here behind those names" (239). On the other hand, Sam also perceives the memorial as being like "a black boomerang ," a "black wing," "the wings of an abstract bird, huge and headless," (239) and "the white wings of the shopping mall in Paducah" (240). The allusions to wings connect with the bird imagery that has connoted transcendence throughout the novel, although here they are ambiguous. The conflicting signifiers of the memorial further unsettle Sam, for although it is monumentally rock-like, the images of its visitors are hauntingly reflected in the polished surfaces of the black granite. She recognizes the indeterminacy of this cultural "text" as the inscriptions of the names of the lost soldiers seem to her to be "A scratching on a rock. Writing. Something for future archaeologists to puzzle over, clues to a language" (244).

As Sam realizes that "she will never really know what happened to all those men in the war," (240) she feels overwhelmed by grief. She has arrived at the memorial having tried unsuccessfully to deny her femininity, aspiring instead to identification with the men in Vietnam. As she mourns, a type of sublime moment occurs in which her identity is almost effaced: she "doesn't understand what she is feeling, but it is something so strong, it is like a tornado moving in her, something massive and overpowering." This is figured in terms of the female "destiny" that she has tried to deny: "It feels like giving birth to this wall" (240). Sam appears to be assuming here the possibility of motherhood, against which she has rebelled until this point. After this, the reconstitution of her identity occurs through various gestures.

She finds her father's name, and the inscription in the granite seems to confer upon it a materiality and a history. She touches the name as though the writing were to replace the lost body. Having found her father's name, she discovers her "own" name, "Sam Alan Hughes," which she touches, feeling as though "all the names in America have been used to decorate the wall" (245).[41] This appears to signify her honorary inclusion among the lost American soldiers and, metonymically, among the "community" of Americans. But despite her sense of recognition, Samantha Hughes's name is not identical to the name on the wall, which suggests that the historical construction of sexual difference cannot be so easily overcome.

Mason's depiction of the scenes at the memorial has provoked some negative critical responses. Some critics have argued that the narrative has a "strongly ameliorative point of view,"[42] which culminates in the concluding scenes, and that this blunts the questions about history, authority, and who has access to them, which are asked elsewhere in the novel. Yonka Krasteva, alluding to the image of the wall that forms the "wings" of the memorial, has noted that Mason creates a "walled-in" structure that implies "a closure" by framing the middle section of the narrative, recounted in the past tense, with the present-tense sections describing the journey to and arrival at the memorial.[43] Similarly, Matthew C. Stewart finds the novel to be flawed by this structure, which suggests "an encouraging account of a healing family, of the reintegration of a troubled veteran into a once careless society, and of reconciliation on both a personal and a societal level." In a novel that generally represents the plight of the veterans with commendable verisimilitude,

Mason should not, he argues, "reverse her course by implying that instantaneous harmonious integration of self and society is somehow possible for a man like Emmett."[44]

Other critics have questioned the erasure of difference[45] that they believe is suggested by Sam's discovery of "her own" name on the wall. James Campbell, in his exploration of issues that are raised by the representation of the reconciliation of veterans and civilians in "narratives of return to 'the World,'" has, on the one hand, commended the "admirable" connotations of Sam's discovery of the name: "All of America, including that part of it barely even born during the war, lived through the war and continues to live with its traces. In a certain sense, we all have a stake in the Wall, and we must all confront it and find our own name on it."[46] But on the other hand, he argues, Samantha's identification with the name may "erase" or "appropriate" "the particularity of Sam Alan Hughes's experience . . . and the death it signifies." "Reconciliation with the veteran," he concludes, cannot be premised upon the assumption that "our cultural struggles with Vietnam make us all casualties of that war."[47] Susan Jeffords's critique of the elision of difference implied by Sam's discovery is made from a different standpoint. According to Jeffords, although Mason has drawn attention throughout the novel to Sam's exclusion, as a woman, from knowledge about the Vietnam War, the narrative suggests that the continuation of this exclusion is necessary to strengthen the masculine bonds—and masculinity—that have been weakened by the "emasculating" treatment of the veterans on their return. Moreover, the concept of collectivity that the novel puts forward is synonymous with the "masculine bond." Following Sam's realization, at Cawood's Pond, that she cannot know what the men knew in Vietnam and her consequent deferral of agency to Emmett as he initiates the trip to the memorial, her honorary inclusion in the masculine community is confirmed by her discovery of her "own" name on the memorial.[48]

Yet, although the main thrust of this scene is to suggest the reestablishment of community through the characters' recognition of a continuity between their personal memories and public history, tensions remain in Mason's evocation of it. The "community" signified here is a provisional one that incorporates renewed familial bonds, although not those of the idealized American nuclear family. The final image of the novel suggests that Mason is not offering an unqualified celebration of the recreation of "community," when the preceding narrative has stressed that the inclusion of some people always depends upon the exclusion of others. Sam watches Emmett scrutinizing the names on the wall: "He is sitting there cross-legged in front of the wall, and slowly his face bursts into a smile like flames" (245). Although this suggests that Sam's vision of Emmett is redemptive and that Emmett has reconciled himself to his losses, Mason's image could also evoke the self-immolation of Buddhist priests in Vietnam in protest against the war, or indeed the immolation of the Vietnamese people and landscape by American technology. This ambiguous image suggests that differences cannot be simply recuperated into a homogenizing American history. Throughout the narrative Sam has rebelled against her difference from the "norm" of white masculinity, at the same time as she has criticized the equation of masculinity with war. The concluding scenes at the memorial show her achieving some acceptance of the "otherness" of her femininity. Emmett has also rebelled against both the cultural construction of masculinity and American exclusions of ethnic otherness,[49] specifically that of the Vietnamese. The concluding image is a reminder that such differences cannot easily be erased or assimilated by a homogenizing "American" culture.

CHAPTER FOUR

Spence + Lila and *Love Life*

In her second novel, *Spence + Lila* (1988), Mason focuses on a couple's memories of farm life in rural Kentucky, presenting an affectionate and sympathetically humorous perspective on a way of life and a landscape that are being eroded by the shopping malls, television culture, and interstates of the 1980s. In "The Way We Lived: The Chicken Tower" Mason observes some of the changes that have occurred in the Jackson Purchase region where she grew up and which is the setting of much of her fiction, including *Spence + Lila*. Mason describes the location of the family farm: "We are within sight of the railroad, which parallels U.S. Highway 45. We're a mile from downtown Mayfield, county seat of Graves County, Kentucky. We are in far-western Kentucky, that toe tip of the state shaped by the curve of the great rivers—the Ohio meets the Mississippi at Cairo, Illinois, about thirty-five miles north-west of Mayfield. To the east, the Tennessee and the Cumberland Rivers (now swelled into T. V. A. lakes) run parallel courses. Water forms this twenty-five-hundred-square-mile region into a peninsula. It's attached to land along the border with Tennessee."[1] Mason's description highlights the characteristics of the region that have influenced her own life and that shape the themes of her fiction: the peninsula, conducive to insularity,[2] is transected by the means of traveling across and out of it. Highway 45, in particular, represented "the allure of rootlessness" to the young Mason.[3] Mason observes that since the time when the settlers first cultivated the land that Andrew Jackson had purchased from Chinubby, king of the Chicasaw Nation, in 1818, the landscape is "still changing."[4] Social change, she has remarked, has occurred slowly, but inevitably: "I've noticed that Kentuckians are generally conservative and skeptical of change until it is all the rage elsewhere. We always seem to be teetering between tradition and inevitability."[5] Mason suggests that "the tension between holding on to a way of life and letting in a new way of life—under the banners of Wal-Marts and chicken-processors—is the central dynamic of this area."[6] She has connected the tension between conservatism and adaptation to change with Kentucky's position as "a border state": "Kentucky has a kind of Janus-faced sense of direction. . . . The climate is both Northern and Southern,"[7] although she has also claimed that the Jackson Purchase region specifically "looks to the South" "historically and temperamentally."[8]

In *Spence + Lila* Mason explores the dynamics of change in her native region by focusing on the thoughts and memories of Spence and Lila Culpepper during the few days Lila spends in a hospital undergoing surgery for cancer.[9] In the foreground Mason depicts her protagonists gaining a strength and an optimism from their memories of a stable life on the farm and the work, routines, and knowledge that have been tied to raising their cattle and cultivating their land. Mason counterpoints these memories with scenes in the hospital, where the Culpeppers represent a modern family characterized by some of the elements of contemporary life that she explores elsewhere in her work.

Mason's style is at its plainest here, as she represents the reflections and homespun wisdom that the Culpeppers have derived from their life on the land. Her evocation of Spence's and Lila's steadfast relationship, anchored by their love of life on their farm, creates an impression of luminous artlessness. This is emphasized by the naive style of the book's cover and illustrations by Bobbie Ann's sister, LaNelle Mason (who also designed the cover of *Love Life*), which here evoke an innocent, childlike view of the people and landscape depicted by the novel. The novel celebrates the Culpeppers' relationship, values, and way of life, although any nostalgia for a culture that is being lost is balanced by Spence's and Lila's realistic view of the past and their embrace of certain aspects of contemporary culture.

In the opening lines Mason describes Spence driving to visit Lila in the hospital in Paducah: "Spence notices the row of signs along the highway: WHERE WILL YOU BE IN ETERNITY? Each word is on a white cross. The message reminds him of the old Burma-Shave signs."[10] These sentences establish Spence's current preoccupation with mortality and his skepticism about the consolations offered by Bible Belt evangelism. The comparison of the crosses to Burma Shave signs shows how Spence's imagination has been permeated by consumer culture, but the allusion to the advertisement of a product that has long since disappeared is also nostalgic. Through the references to both the Burma Shave signs and the crosses, Mason shows how Spence's imagination has been shaped by a distinctive regionalism that, as the novel will describe, is being eroded by the industrialization of the landscape and the spread of an "American" consumer culture.[11]

Mason sketches the effect of recent changes even on the sanctum of home and family as the Culpeppers gather around

Lila's bedside. The Culpepper children have dispersed as a result of education and geographical and class mobility: Spence observes that "His family is busting out at the seams. . . . He can't keep track of what they are up to" (47). Nancy Culpepper, the eldest daughter, has flown to Kentucky from Boston, where she "has an important job—something to do with computers—with a company that requires her to travel all over the United States" (45). Nancy, who reappears here from "Nancy Culpepper" and "Lying Doggo," left home for college and married "a Yankee." Spence reflects that "she was always restless and adventurous, because of the books she read" (46). Nancy has also espoused some of the ideas of Women's Liberation, as represented by the fact that when she "moved up north she stopped wearing lipstick and curling her hair, and for a while she didn't even wear a brassiere" (42). The life of her younger sister, Cat, is also alien to her parents: Lila worries about "the way she has been running around with men she hardly knows since her divorce last year" (17). Spence and Lila have had to sell their cattle, and their son, Lee, tries to persuade Spence that he is "setting on a gold mine" (100) and should sell his land so that a subdivision can be developed there. Lee, however, is struggling to support his family and to "keep up his house and car payments" (22). Spence and Lila witness these changes in their modern family with resignation. However, they regard the effects of the transformations of the Kentucky landscape as more invidious. Spence thinks of how "wildcats scavenged at the dump beyond the industrial park" (33), and Lila "puffs away like the smoke-stack in the industrial park beyond the soybean fields. . . . they are like coordinated events in his life, events he has no control over" (52). The devastation of the natural landscape wrought by the industrial park is signified by the fact that "most of the songbirds have disappeared" since it was built (117). His friend Bill, who "hasn't grown tobacco since the bottom fell out of the burley market," (115) is growing marijuana among his soybeans because "besides the crop duster plane, Bill is deeply in debt for a combine and a planter" (76). In addition, the effects of a fire in the tobacco warehouse have killed the fish in the creek, and the trees on Spence's farm have been burned by pesticide.

However, while these changes occur around them, Spence's and Lila's marriage and their love of each other and the farm provide stability. At the heart of Mason's evocation of the Culpeppers' relationship is her representation of Lila's body, as Lila experiences it and Spence perceives it. In contrast to *In Country,* which explores its adolescent protagonist's ambivalence toward motherhood, *Spence + Lila* celebrates the fertile, reproductive, and nurturing maternal body. Its abundance parallels that of the land. Spence tells Lila that "her breasts are like cow bags," and he "has funny names for them, like the affectionate names he had for his cows when they used to keep milk cows," (19) and for Lila, "the tugging sensation of nursing them [her children] is as clear as yesterday" (86). But just as industrialization has scarified the landscape, so Lila's breast cancer seems to her "to suggest some basic failing, like the rotten core of a dying tree" (30).

Spence and Lila are sustained in their confrontation with Lila's mortality by their reminiscences, which pervade the narrative. These memories, which are sharply differentiated along gender lines, hark back to times when gender roles were clearly defined, as were the responsibilities, values, and forms of knowl-

edge attached to the family, community, and labor. The Culpeppers' memories are not nostalgic, however, as they focus on
hardship as well as pleasure. Spence has been haunted by his
memories of serving on a battleship in the Pacific during the Second World War, when he consoled himself by thinking "about
Lila, nursing the baby and helping his parents get the crops in"
(48). After the war Spence, unable to sleep, "stayed up late and
read about the battles," (77) but "the more he read, the more con-
fusing it became, the larger it grew" (78). Lila's memories of this
period are of the hardship she endured caring for a baby while
she lived with Spence's parents, Amp and Rosie. She recalls a
house that "was dark and filled with silences" (70) and the harsh-
ness of women's work in the farm kitchen: "Rosie washed dishes
in an enamel pan set on a gas ring and scalded them in another
pan on another ring. The scum of the slippery lye soap never
really washed off the dishes. Rosie added the dirty dishwater to
the slop bucket for the hogs. Hogs liked the taste, she said. That
fall, a neighbor helped Amp butcher a hog and Rosie made lye
soap from the fat. Lila sewed sausage casings from floursacks.
She added flecks of dried peppers to the ground sausage" (25).
This hardship was compounded by having to nurse the baby,
Nancy, through pneumonia with only "heated bricks wrapped in
newspaper" to warm the bed and "greased rags" to wrap her
chest because they could not afford to pay a doctor to treat her
(26). Spence's parents' home was a patriarchal domain where
Amp whipped his granddaughter for disobedience. Lila concludes, retrospectively, that men "had a secret, awful power"
(142). Lila's memories of her own childhood, although affectionate, do not provide an idealized view of the past, either. She

recalls how, after her father "abandoned her when she was four and went off to Alaska," (23), she was taken into her Uncle Mose's extended family: "It shot off in different directions—in-laws, cousins, widows, a cousin with an illegitimate child, an aunt whose husband had abandoned her. Uncle Mose took in strays like Lila, anybody with a pair of hands to help him work his tobacco" (70).

The effect of their gender roles upon Spence and Lila, as well as their temperamental differences, has led them to adapt differently to aging. Spence reflects that "when he got home from the Navy, she seemed stronger, tougher, and he felt weaker, torn apart" (77). Mason returns to her exploration of why people choose to stay at home, leave, or return as she contrasts Spence's with Lila's responses to advancing age. New opportunities are opened up after the death of Spence's mother, for whom Lila has cared for years, and they have raised their children and sold their cattle. Since the war Spence has not wanted to travel again, but Lila has rejoiced in her trips to "Hawaii, the Badlands, Savannah and New Orleans" with the senior citizens (36). She reflects that "she was seeing what Spence saw in the Navy, and maybe seeing what Nancy was looking for when she left home" (140).

Both Spence and Lila have embraced what they regard as the positive aspects of social change, without discarding their old values. Cat tells her mother "everything's different now, and you don't know how hard it is to work it all out. Things aren't the way they used to be—if they ever *were*" (107–8). Lila, however, recalls how she worked at a clothing factory to buy basic commodities while also raising her children and working on the farm. She remembers how her work at the factory made her feel "proud and alive. It was piecework, and sometimes she could make nearly ninety cents an hour, she was so fast," (88) yet she tells her daughters "times are better now. . . . You don't know how good you've got it" (87).

As in *Shiloh,* Mason's representation of the rituals surrounding the preparation and consumption of food is a central indicator of the changes wrought by consumer culture on traditional ways of life. For Lila, tending her garden and preparing its produce in her kitchen are life-affirming activities that mark the passage of time and the changing seasons. The traditional rituals of a residual community are evinced as neighbors bring Spence food they have prepared for him while Lila is in the hospital: "an odd assortment of dishes—coconut pie, lima beans cooked with macaroni, stewed tomatoes, green Jell-O streaked with shredded cabbage" (75). Nonetheless, Spence and Lila derive pleasure from fast food and its associated commodities: Spence has contrived his own ritual around cooking breakfast in the microwave, and he recalls how, "when he and Lila were courting," "a hamburger and Coke at Fred and Sue's Drive-in was the most delicious meal they had ever had. . . . His mother was stingy with meat and cooked the same plain grub day in and day out" (99–100).

The rock and roll that Spence listens to as he drives to and from the hospital is both a source of pleasure to him and a means of interpreting social transformation: "The music fits the urgency of his life. The music seems to organize all the noises of public places into something he can tolerate" (46). The value of this music and its meaningfulness to him have their roots in his memory, which again revolves around an image of Lila: "Before the children were born, he and Lila used to go dancing at little places out in the country that people called 'nigger juke joints.' . . . He can imagine her long legs now, flashing white in the dark of the dance floor. . . . The real music is always hidden somewhere, off in the country, back in his head, in his memory" (46). Television has similarly become woven into the Culpeppers' daily lives. As Lila regains consciousness, she tries to focus on a soap opera that is playing on the ward television, and Spence discusses a baseball game with other viewers. One of the most poignantly joyful moments in the novel occurs as Lila regains consciousness after her operation. Spence, who recalls "dancing with Cat to Ike and Tina Turner and the Ikettes on the radio," (159) shows her Mick Jagger and Tina Turner dancing on the television (160). Both Lila and Spence believe that television has produced positive social changes. Lila remembers how the acquisition of their first television filled their household of young children with "an unexpected harmony." She reflects upon how the family gathering around *I Love Lucy* contrasted favorably with "long winter nights at Uncle Mose's, when there was no entertainment to work by" (83). Similarly, Spence believes that television enables him " "to see places he'd never go to" and that "his grandchildren are smart because of all they are exposed to on TV" (157).

The Culpepper family's various perceptions of the scenes in the hospital further illustrate the effects of recent changes. Lila, recalling her battle to save her daughter from pneumonia before penicillin was invented, welcomes the developments of medical science, but her more educated daughters are skeptical about the way doctors use specialized and alienating terminology to guard their own knowledge and authority. To Lila, however, whose "innocence has always embarrassed her," her children also possess "strange knowledge," such as "cholesterol, women's rights" (139). Nancy experiences a moment of self-consciousness when she realizes that she is using a discourse that might be alien and intrusive to her father. She explains: "'Mom doesn't want us to think she's not strong and positive. It's her maternal instinct. She can't stop protecting us, even when she has been violated in the worst way," but to Spence's embarrassment, she stops, "as if she thinks Spence might not understand her words" (127).

In his review of *Spence + Lila* and *Love Life,* Devon Jersild notes that "some critics have charged that Mason condescends to her characters, that she portrays them as confused, uneducated, lower-middle-class types who are trapped in their pain because they don't have the tools to understand their dilemmas, while she and the reader look on with superior understanding." But, he argues, "I do not believe that she implies a causal relation between emotional clumsiness and social class."[12] *Spence + Lila* offers a moving defense of its protagonists' perceptions and shows how their apparent "inarticulateness" is derived from the values of their culture. Spence, who is irritated by the doctors' use of specialized terminology, reflects that he "knows big words, plenty of them. He prefers not to use his vocabulary in conversation, though, for fear of sounding pretentious. Using the right simple words at the right time requires courage enough. At times there is no way on earth he can say what he feels" (73). To try and express his feelings for Lila would seem "phony. . . . like something on television," but "everything he does is for her, even when he goes his own way and she is powerless to stop him" (73). The "phoniness" of a culture that demands the expression of one's feelings is illustrated by the letters and pamphlets that a woman from "the mastectomy support group" gives to Lila to send to members of her family, articulating for her what she might feel as a result of the operation. She reads in one of the pamphlets, for example: "'Women usually go through a period of depression after a mastectomy. They equate their femininity and their sexuality with their lost breast'" (112). The discourse here does not communicate the feelings Lila would wish to express to her relatives.

Mason attributes some of the most beautifully lyrical passages in the novel to Spence and Lila. The hope and optimism expressed in these passages is derived from their knowledge of the land and natural cycles of renewal. Elsewhere, Mason has reflected on the disappearance of forms of knowledge, memory, and language bound to labor on the land, as she surveys the family farm after the death of her father: "I think about what a farmer knows up there on his tractor or walking behind his mules—the slow, enduring pace of regular toil and the habit of mind that goes with it, the habit of knowing what is lasting and of noting every nuance of soil and water and season. What my father and my ancestors knew has gone, and their language lingers like relics. Soon my memories will be loosened from any tangible connection to this land."[13] Writing of *Spence + Lila,* Devon Jersild has observed that "Mason's idealizations . . . say less about the past itself than about the modern longing for a life in harmony with nature, a time and place where one's work provided satisfying metaphors of self in relation to the world."[14] For example, as Lila struggles to articulate to herself her thoughts about "growing into old age toward death," she believes "there is something important about movement she wants to tell." Her observations of nature provide her with a language for her thoughts: "The way corn will shoot up after a rain. The way a baby chicken's feathers start showing. The way a pair of wrens will worry and worry with a pile of sticks, determined that the place they have chosen is the right one for a nest" (140). Mason accords a similar passage of serene acceptance, grounded in his relation to nature, to Spence, as he looks out over his farm: "This is it. This is all there is in the world—it contains everything there is to know or possess, yet everywhere people are knocking their brains out trying to find something different, something better. His kids all scattered, looking for it. Everyone always wants a way out of something like this, but what he has here is the main thing there is—just the way things grow and die, the way the sun comes up and goes down every day. These are the facts of life. They are so simple they are almost impossible to grasp" (133).

Spence's perception of the landscape fuses with his memories of Lila's body, expressing his joy at the vitality of both, as in: "He can still see her short, loose dress, her breasts swinging like fruit on a branch in a strong breeze" (79). As Lila undergoes her operations, her wounded body is mapped onto the ravaged landscape through Spence's eyes: "On the edge of the field, he steps across a ridge of dirt pushed up by a tractor tire. A few stray soybeans perch on the top, and the tire print beside it is dry like a scar. He thinks of the furrows the doctors may cut in Lila's neck" (76). Spence's conflation of Lila's body with the land increases as he awaits her return. As he flies over the farm in Bill's plane, he gains a new perspective on his land, amusing himself with the idea that "the woods are like hair, the two creeks like the parting of a woman's legs, the house and barn her nipples" (164). These rather banal similes are, however, regenerated by a comparison informed by his own loving observation of the detail of his land when he looks at Lila in their garden: "Her face is rosy, all the furrows and marks thrusting upward with her smile the way the okra on the stalk reach upward toward the sun. Her face is as pretty as freshly plowed ground, and the scar on her neck is like a gully washed out but filling in now" (175). Ultimately, the effect of such associations, which pervade the novel, is not to sublimate either Lila's body or the landscape into metaphors but rather to ground the presence of both against the cultural changes occurring elsewhere. The celebration that Mason offers in *Spence + Lila* of her protagonists' love and desire for each other, and of the optimism they derive from the natural cycles that shape their life on the farm, is epitomized by the novel's final, affirmatory image: "Her cough catches her finally and slows her down, but her face is dancing like pond water in the rain, all unsettled and stirring with aroused possibility" (176).

In *Spence + Lila* Mason's depiction of the encroachments of contemporary culture upon traditional ways of life is etched lightly upon the vitality of remembered lives, but in her next work, *Love Life* (1989), Mason focuses on the difficulty of loving and "loving life" in a contemporary culture whose subjects feel alienated from the self and society. This collection of short stories, set mainly in western Kentucky, is unified by themes familiar from Mason's earlier fiction, such as the "culture shock" and sense of exile experienced by her characters as the traditions of rural life are eroded by consumer culture and the effect on her characters' sense of identity of such "democratizing" discourses as education, feminism, and the interpretations of life offered by television. Within individual stories, these "themes" are frequently only glimpsed through allusive images, narrative suggestion, and partial characterization. Lorrie Moore has observed in her review of the stories that "many of the stories in *Love Life* splay out unexpectedly, skate off, or in, at odd angles, displaying a directional looseness. . . . Certainly the beginnings and endings do illuminate each other, but only indirectly, diffusely. Along the way elements are seldom developed in a linear fashion, and are often, once introduced, abandoned altogether."[15] Moore comments that the overall effect of the stories, however, is one of "cumulative beauty," the achievement of "accumulation, a supply," as each story offers a meditation on the possibility, or failure, of different types of love in small-town Kentucky. Through the form of "the story *collection,*" Moore remarks, "Mason depicts most richly a community of contemporary lives, which is her great skill."[16] Such "community" is largely unrecognized by its members but is constructed between the author and her readers as the repetition of stylistic, structural, and thematic elements, often with unexpected variations, enables the reader to perceive common concerns among the characters. Whereas Moore discerns a cumulative "depth" and "profundity" in *Love Life,* Devon Jersild remarks that a "cool surface" is produced by Mason's tendency "to refrain from comment, extrapolations, conclusions."[17] In *Love Life,* Jersild argues, this "authorial restraint mirrors her characters' distance from emotion and produces a certain numbing effect."[18]

Many of the characters in *Love Life,* as in *Shiloh,* are locked in the present moment. As Lorrie Moore has put it, Mason's "use of the present tense in the majority of her stories serves as the expression of [their] trapped condition, but also as a kind of existential imperfect: the freeze in time suggests the flow; the moment stilled and isolated from the past and future is yet emblematic of them both, of the gray ongoingness of things."[19] In several of the stories, Mason explores the effect of the past on the present, as her characters attempt to reconcile them through the process of mourning, whereby a grieving for cultural losses is incorporated into personal mourning. In contrast to *In Country,* the stories express little movement toward closure of the process of mourning, although there are occasional glimpses of the possibility of personal or cultural "healing." This lack of closure is emphasized by Mason's use of the short story form: the open endings reveal little sense of how to move from the present into the future.

In the title story, which opens the collection, Mason focuses on the sympathetic cross-generational relationship between Opal and her niece, Jenny. Opal, a retired schoolteacher, has adjusted to her increased leisure time by enjoying the escapist fantasies stimulated by watching MTV and listening to rock and roll. Never having "cared for stories," Opal is mesmerized by the way in which "the colors and the costumes change and flow with the music, erratically, the way her mind does these days."[20] These rapidly changing images allow her to remain in a fluid present, where she does not need to rely for sustenance on the impoverished memories of a past constrained by provincial censoriousness about the behavior appropriate to a single woman.[21] It quickly becomes clear, however, that Jenny feels more adrift.

Having availed herself of the social changes for women that have occurred between Opal's generation and hers, Jenny has been waitressing in Denver. But, in another variation on the theme of staying at home, leaving, or returning, Jenny "was growing restless again, and the idea of going home seized her. Her old rebellion against small-town conventions gave way to curiosity" (3). Back in Kentucky, Jenny pursues her fantasy of recovering her roots as she dates a local man, Randy Newcomb, and buys a plot of land because she wants "a remote place where she can have a dog and grow some tomatoes" (5). Jenny's sense of exile from the "home" to which she has returned creates a feeling of culture shock through which the South is rendered strange: "In the South, the shimmer of the heat seems to distort everything, like old glass with impurities in it" (3). Her estrangement from the South makes its seem grotesque as, in her first two days there, her attention is drawn to "two people with artificial legs, a blind man, a man with hooks for hands, and a man without an arm" (3). Sensitive to her own difference, she imagines herself becoming a grotesque spectacle, fantasizing about being attacked by a pit bull "in an arena, with a crowd watching." Although Randy Newcomb tells her "we're not as countrified down here now as people think," Jenny perceives the local people as types, noticing that there were "two kind of women" in a bar she visits, which makes her feel "odd" as "she was neither type" (4).

It becomes apparent that Jenny's estrangement from her surroundings is part of a process of mourning for personal and cultural losses. This association of mourning with a defamiliarizing perception and a sense of the grotesque recurs throughout the collection. In "Love Life" Jenny's attempt to recover her "roots" and connect herself with the past becomes increasingly focused on her aunt's collection of crazy quilts, and the family burial quilt in particular. This "dark and somber" quilt is comprised of blocks, on each of which "is an appliqued off-white tombstone— a comical shape, like Casper the ghost. Each tombstone has a name and date on it" (14). Opal, who tells Jenny "I try to be modern," (10) refuses to romanticize the women's history, community, and labor represented by the quilt. She is happy to pass the "burden" of the quilt on to her niece, as it signifies to her "miserable, cranky women, straining their eyes, stitching on those dark scraps of material" (16). The communal rite of mourning represented by the quilt prompts Jenny to tell her aunt that she has just received news of the death of a former lover with whom she had lost touch. The isolation of the contemporary subject through geographic mobility, historical dislocation, and transient social relationships, unrecognized by ritual or tradition, is articulated in Jenny's explanation that "If I still knew him, I would know how to mourn, but now I don't know how. And it was over a year ago. So now I don't know what to feel" (17). The story ends ambiguously as Opal consoles herself with the alternating fantasies of violence and sexual freedom on her television: an image of "smoke emerg[ing] from an eyeball," which may belong to "a woman . . . lying on her stomach on a car hood in a desert full of gas pumps," (17) segues into a classroom scene of pupils "gyrating and snapping their fingers to wild music" (18). Opal, whose image of her own "freedom" is signified by a memory of a liaison with a man in a motel room "devoid of history and association," (11) in Nashville, fantasizes that "the teacher is thinking about how, when the bell rings, she will hit the road to Nashville" (18).

Mason returns to her exploration of mourning in a culture of transient relationships in "The Secret of the Pyramids." Barbara's married former lover has just been killed in a car crash. Her friend tells her that "you have to work out your grief somehow," but Barbara responds: "Grief? . . . Is that what it is? Yesterday I hated him, and today I feel—I don't know what" (71). Isolated from a community of mourners that would publicly recognize her bereavement, Barbara is unable to interpret the past in a way that would make sense of the present. She fondly recalls visiting Cairo, Illinois, with her lover and his story about how "young boys come to Cairo . . . to learn the secret of the pyramids," (73) but this fragment of historical lore remains extraneous to her understanding of her own culture. Her sense of being stranded in the present is heightened by her perception of the alienating nature of the shopping mall where she works and where her lover owned a store: "It is the only quality mall for more than a hundred miles, and people from the country and the small towns congregate here on the weekend. . . . Everyone looks dazed" (76). Dissociated from her own grief, Barbara witnesses how the process of mourning has become a public spectacle. As she reads in the newspaper about the death of her lover, she observes that "in print, he was a distant figure, like a celebrity" (77), and visiting the funeral home, she approaches his body "lying in the casket like a store display" (79). At the end of the story, Barbara "locates his traces" in the only private tokens of the relationship that she possesses: the memorabilia she has collected on her travels with him. The concluding image reveals how, fittingly, all that she keeps from these is an icon of the com-modification of another figure by consumer culture: a "pink Elvis Presley clock shaped like a guitar" (80–1).

Mason returns to explore the dislocation of the subject that grief produces in "Bumblebees." Ruth, whose husband and daughter have been killed in a car crash, and Barbara, who is divorced, are trying to "rebuild their lives" in a house in the country. Barbara attempts to restore herself by working in the garden, and Ruth is "working on quilt pieces" (105). Barbara's daughter, Allison, has returned, changed, from college and is "trying to get centered" (103). Each day Allison "brings in some treasure: the cracked shell of a freckled sparrow egg, a butterfly wing," and Barbara believes that "her daughter, deprived of so much of the natural world during her childhood in town, is going through a delayed phase of discovery now" (104). Despite their attempts to replenish themselves through their contact with nature, each of the women continues to feel dissociated from herself. Ruth has thrown away the photographs of her dead husband and child because, as she explains, "one day I realized that I knew the faces in the pictures better than I knew my memories of their faces" (105). Barbara also experiences moments of detachment from herself, as for example, when she "sees the three of them, on the porch on that hillside, as though they were in a painting. . . . Barbara sees herself in her garden, standing against her hoe handle like a scarecrow at the mercy of the breezes that barrel over the ridge" (107).

Throughout the story the women's relation to the house and garden that they are attempting to restore serves as a symbol for their continuing grief and alienation. The floor of an upper room of the house is covered with dead bumblebees, and live bees torment the women. The garden supplies Barbara with a metaphor with which to interpret her situation: "She had the feeling that she was tending too many gardens; everything around her was growing in some sick or stunted way, and it made her feel cramped" (112). Her sense of dislocation also defamiliarizes the landscape around the house. In a moment reminiscent of Raymond Carver's stories, Barbara's perception of her ordinary, everyday environment is profoundly unsettled: "But sometimes it suddenly all seems strange, like something she has never seen before. . . . in this light, with this particular dog, with his frayed bandage, and that particular stick and the wet grass that needs mowing—it is something Barbara has never seen before in her life" (113). Mason does, however, imply some movement toward healing through her focalizing character's perception of images associated with the house and garden. As Barbara continues to walk through the woods, she notices "a fantastic array of mushrooms": "The mushrooms are so unexpected, it is as though they had grown up in a magical but clumsy compensation for the ruined garden" (113). The story concludes with Allison teasing the distressed Ruth that the bundle of rags she has found in the attic contains a dead baby. Barbara, who realizes the rags are just "old stockings with runs," watches her daughter burn them: "The smell of burning dust is very precise. It is like the essence of the old house. It is concentrated filth, and Allison is burning it up for them" (115).

In "Big Bertha Stories" Mason again explores the suffering of a Vietnam veteran and his relatives.[22] The story is told from the point of view of Jeanette, who is married to a veteran, Donald. Donald spends most of his time away from home, working at a strip mine in Muhlenberg County,[23] occasionally returning "like an absentee landlord checking on his property" (116). In this story, as in *In Country,* Mason evokes some of the symptoms of trauma presented by the veterans: Donald suffers from depression, nightmares, and a sense of meaninglessness. He tells his son, Rodney, "strange stories" about "Big Bertha," the name he has given to the strip-mining machine, informing Rodney that "Big Bertha is just like a wonderful woman, a big fat woman who can sing the blues" (120). Rodney "loves the stories," but the phantasmagoric images of Big Bertha return in his dreams and the troubled pictures he draws. Jeanette regularly visits a therapist whom she calls "The Rapist," and she feels "her family disintegrating like a spider shattering" (117).

When he first went to work at the strip mine, Donald tried to explain to Jeanette how the American despoliation of Vietnam was like strip mining: "America was just stripping off the top, the best. We ruined it," (118) but such accounts have been replaced by the Big Bertha stories. However, in this story, as in *In Country,* the veteran's expression of silenced memories leads to his desire to find resolution of a grief that has remained open since the war. Donald tells of meeting a Vietnamese woman, Phan, who "was beautiful, like the country," and of how he did not know what happened to her because although the "jungle was the most beautiful place in the world. . . . we blew it sky-high" (130). "Big Bertha" has become a hallucinatory configuration that fuses the destructive power of American technology, the luxuriance and devastation of the Vietnamese landscape, and the bodies of the Vietnamese women whom the American soldiers desired and killed. Donald's articulation of his sense of guilt enables him to agree to undergo treatment in the Veterans Hospital. While he is there, Jeanette gets a job and recognizes what her own expectations of Donald have been: "she has thought of Donald primarily as a husband, a provider, someone whose name she shared, the father of her child" (131). Despite the increased self-reflection of both characters, the story ends ambiguously. Jeanette buys a trampoline for Rodney and imagines herself on it when Donald returns "and sees her flying," an image of apparent freedom. But Donald's troubled memories seem to haunt her own dreams as "that night, she has a nightmare about the trampoline. In her dream she is jumping on soft moss, and then it turns into a springy pile of dead bodies" (132).

An adolescent's first encounter with bereavement is one of the themes of "State Champions." The frame of the story is one of cultural loss, emphasizing the disjuncture between past and present. The story opens with the narrator recounting how "in 1952, when I was in the seventh grade, the Cuba Cubs were the state champions in high-school basketball" (133). The narrator recalls how, twenty years later, she met a Kentuckian in upstate New York who pointed out that the Cuba Cubs were "just a handful of country boys who could barely afford basketball shoes" (134). To the child, Peggy, these boys were "the essence of glamour" (135), and in part her story recounts the awakening of desire through her infatuation with one of the players. But the Kentuckian's comment has prompted her to reinterpret her history, and the story changes direction, as, interpolated into her memories, is the recollection of hearing the news of the death of her best friend's sister. She recalls her self-consciousness in the presence of her bereaved friend, who seems to have "some secret knowledge that lifted her above us" (144). Desire is superseded by awe of death and bereavement as she approaches her celebrating hero: "I wanted to tell him what it was like to be at home when such a terrible thing happened, but I couldn't" (144). The story is tinged with nostalgia for a rural childhood, but it evokes the loss of innocence through an awakening self-consciousness accompanied by increased social sophistication.

A sense of loss informs the remainder of the stories in the collection, where Mason explores the difficulty of sustaining relationships in an alienating culture. Here, as in *Shiloh,* Mason examines the effect of changing gender roles on working-class men. This is the focus of one of the more disturbing stories in the collection, "Midnight Magic," which begins with the protagonist, Steve, reflecting on how, "prowling in his car ['Midnight Magic'] at night, he could be Dracula" (19). In the introduction to *Midnight Magic: Selected Stories of Bobbie Ann Mason,* Mason has elaborated on both the significance of the title story and her conception of the writing process. She comments on her empathy with the protagonist of the "Midnight Magic," explaining that "The mystery of writing is much like driving into the darkness in the middle of the night. It's both dangerous and fraught with possibility. After all, the nighttime is double-edged. It may be the dark night of the soul, but it's also night life: the time for seduction and transformation—the creation of magic." Further, Mason comments: "When I wrote these stories, I was venturing along roads that looked familiar, but which I found myself seeing in a new way. I discovered that a backlog of imagery is stored in the dark recesses of the mind, as if waiting to emerge at night—like Dracula. That's what the creative act is for me—a challenge to inhibition, a delving into the hidden and forgotten."[24]

Mason's identification with her protagonist's fascination with the darkness, and her association of the creative process with the retrieval of what lies hidden in "the dark recesses of the mind," offer some insight into the ambiguous tone she sustains throughout "Midnight Magic." She has also commented on the development of her characterization of Steve, explaining that the story "was inspired by a guy I saw sitting in a car eating chocolate-covered doughnuts and drinking chocolate milk. . . . While I was writing it I couldn't make the person I had seen follow through in my imagination. The real person looked like he could be a rapist and really mean. But I couldn't write him that way. I made him a whole lot nicer that I thought he would be. . . ."[25] The imaginative tensions with which Mason wrestled in writing the story remain imprinted on it. The unsettling ambiguity of "Midnight Magic" is produced by the discrepancy that Mason reveals between Steve's point of view, through which it is the world that seems strange, and other characters' perceptions of Steve's actions, whereby it is his behavior that seems at best misguided and at worst menacing. This discrepancy is mirrored by Steve's sense of dissociation from himself, as is indicated, for example, by his observation that "He has on running shoes, but he was sure he had put on boots. He touches his face. He hasn't shaved" (19). These sentences immediately establish the disjuncture between what Steve thinks he has done and what he has actually done, or failed to do.

Through Steve's eyes the solace that popular culture offers

its alienated subjects seems increasingly bizarre. His girlfriend, Karen, seeks spiritual guidance at meetings held by "Sardo," who is "a thousand-year-old American Indian inhabiting the body of a teenage girl in Paducah," (21) while his jailed father has been converted by TV evangelism. The story acquires a Carveresque inflection as Steve's sense of the oddness of his culture becomes tinged with an undertone of violence. While Steve's girlfriend, Karen, lives in fear of a rapist who is striking in her neighborhood, Steve alarms a woman in the laundromat as he scrutinizes her laundry, and he frightens Karen by pretending he is the rapist. What Steve considers to be an affectionate embrace Karen perceives as what "cats do . . . when they want to rip out a rabbit's guts" (20). As Steve fantasizes about how, if he were the rapist, he would lay in wait for Karen, the reader is led to wonder whether this is the disorientation produced by a seemingly random and at times violent culture upon an impressionable man or whether Steve has become so alienated that he cannot discern the bounds of acceptable behavior. Albert Wilhelm notes that "the rapist . . . lingers as an ominous echo—the penumbral image of an identity that Steve has barely avoided."[26]

Steve's sense of being "empty inside, doomed" (21), resonates with Karen's observation about an albino deer: "'It was like something all bleached out. It wasn't all *there*'" (30). The end of the story emphasizes Steve's immobilizing detachment from his surroundings and his inability to feel the appropriate emotional response to people or situations. Driving along the interstate, he sees what he thinks is a dead man at the side of the road. He drives past, unable to respond, but eventually does report the sighting. The final image is ambiguous, however. Suspended in midconversation in the telephone booth, he observes the car, which symbolizes the latent power he feels he lacks: "His muffler has been growing throatier, making an impressive drag-race rumble. It's the power of Midnight Magic, the sound of his heart" (32).

Mason evokes this sense of dissociation again in "Private Lies," the story of Mickey, who is married to Tina but begins an affair with his ex-wife, Donna. Mickey's betrayal of his wife is informed by his mourning for the daughter whom he and Donna gave up for adoption before they married. While Tina becomes "uncharacteristically helpless," Mickey persuades Donna to accompany him to Florida to search for their daughter. The concluding images evoke how his optimism about the future depends upon his freeing himself from what he regards as the deathly burden of his personal history. As he looks out at the ocean, "he felt, with a sense of relief, that nothing private was left here." He imagines walking along the beach with Donna in the future: "They stepped back, then forward, like dancers. They were moving like this along the beach, crunching the fragments of skeletons" (160).

A sense of the dissociation of the self in an alienating culture also pervades "Piano Fingers" and "Coyotes," but Mason also hints here at the transformative potential of love. In "Piano Fingers" the twenty-six-year-old, unemployed Dean "feels suspended somewhere between childhood and old age, not knowing which direction he is facing" (84). Dean is a dreamer who fantasizes about opening an ice-cream parlor or attending a seminar in real-estate investment, but he realizes that he is adrift. While Dean dreams, his wife, Nancy, who "expects more of him than he has been able to give,"(84) "zooms through" "Bodice Busters" and yearns for her "dream-house" in the new subdivision. Nancy informs him that "it makes her feel powerless not to be in charge of certain things" (92). Dean's sense of dislocation is mirrored in his pessimistic vision of his culture. As he sits in his car in a subdivision, he reflects that "on this street in the last couple of years one man, a school-board member, was arrested for molesting a child at the playground; a young woman tried to commit suicide; a child died of leukemia" (96). However, Mason attributes to Dean both a heightened reflectiveness and a redeeming love for his children. He observes that "the sound of wet leaves against the car on a late-autumn day makes him feel nostalgia for something, he can't remember what. He realizes that there are such moments, such sensations, that are maybe not memory but just things happening now, things that come into focus suddenly and can be either happy or sad" (88). Like many of Mason's characters, Dean believes that "there are too many choices." However, Dean makes a choice, although one he can ill afford. His daughter's piano teacher tells her that she has "piano fingers," which Dean regards as " a God-given talent." He buys her an electronic keyboard, and as he sits watching her with a sense of wonder, "she seems like someone he has suddenly dreamed into reality. He can hardly believe his eyes" (98).

Cobb, the protagonist of "Coyotes," feels that he has been changed by meeting his girlfriend, Lynnette Johnson. He recalls how, in his childhood, "his mother didn't read much. She was always too tired. She worked at a clothing store, and his dad drove a bread truck. There were four children. Nobody ever did anything especially outrageous or strange" (165–66). Lynnette, however, has "made him feel there were different ways to look at the world," and together they find "the unusual in the everyday" (164). Cobb's increased sensitivity to ordinary life defamiliarizes "the everyday," revealing, for example, the disturbing flatness of situations where one might expect to find emotional investment. He is haunted by a "strange scene in a Wal-Mart," where he witnessed two teenagers telling the clerk that they had married. Cobb is "confused," wondering "why weren't these three young people excited and happy?" (167). As in "Midnight Magic," Mason hints at a connection between a pervasive cultural lack of affect and contemporary violence. Lynette, who works in a "film developing place," breaches social etiquette at dinner with Cobb's parents by telling them about how photographs of the victims of violent death are "all mixed in with vacations and children." She comments that "the thing is, they're not unusual at all. They're everywhere, all the time. It's life" (173). Cobb gains some insight into this "morbid" trait of Lynnette's character when she tells him how she fears becoming like her mother, whose psychological illness led to her suicide attempt. The conclusion of this story suggests the redemptive possibility of love, however, as it focuses on Cobb's transfiguring perception. As they watch a feather floating in the creek, Cobb "tried to comprehend all that might happen to that feather as it wore away to bits—a strange thought. In a dozen years, he thought, he might look back on this moment and know that it was precisely when he should have stopped and made a rational decision to go no further, but he couldn't know that now." But, as he watches Lynnette, he realizes that "she couldn't see the way the light came through her hair like the light in spring through a leaving tree" (179).

Other stories in the collection also explore various types of loss associated with recent social changes. In "Marita," for instance, a mother tries to persuade her daughter to terminate her pregnancy so that she will "have choices." The daughter reluctantly agrees, but the story depicts her sense of grief after the termination as she retreats into a protective world of childlike fantasy, which she inhabits with her mother's cats: "We're like the Borrowers. . . . We're tiny and quiet, living in the cabbage roses" (65–66). The narrative withholds judgment about Marita's decision but ends on a positive note as she recalls how she smashed the "flour baby" that she and her fellow schoolgirls were required to make "to teach us the responsibility of having a baby": "I ran away from the gym, tracking flour down the sidewalk, out into the soccer field where I ran free—like a young dog after a flying Frisbee, like someone in love" (67).

Another story that ponders recent changes, especially the effect of feminism on relations between men and women, is "Hunktown." Here, Mason depicts the strain placed on Joann's and Cody's marriage when the unemployed Cody decides to pursue his dream of playing in a band in Nashville. As a waitress in the bar where Cody is playing explains to Joann that she had her "tubes tied" because "I hate it when people *assume* . . . that I'm the one to make supper because I've got reproductive organs," (45) Joann concludes that the waitress "should have sung a song about it, instead of getting herself butchered" (46). Angry as Joann is that she must look on "like an innocent bystander" (51) while the middle-aged Cody irresponsibly pursues his dreams, she can distinguish between "his wild side [and] the part she loved" (53). The concluding image suggests her recognition that she must not neglect this love: "On the porch, the impatiens in a hanging basket had died in the recent freeze. She had forgotten to bring the plant inside. Now she watched it sway and twist in a little whirl of wind" (53). "Airwaves" also traces the disintegration of a relationship after the male partner has become unemployed. When the protagonist, Jane, is also made unemployed, she refuses to let her partner return to support her. Her espousal of "freedom" is troubled, however. She buys a "travel kit" but "wasn't sure where she was going" (195). The conclusion of the story evokes her loneliness as, returning to her apartment for some laundry, she realizes that "she has left the radio on, and for a moment on the landing she thinks that someone must be home" (197).

In "Sorghum" Liz, who believes she has "something like a commuter marriage," searches for "roots" in traditional culture by going to see an old man making sorghum molasses. His son, Ed, informs her, however, that his father "could do everything the old way. But he doesn't have to anymore" (203). Liz begins an affair with Ed, but her sense of having lost her roots becomes more acute as she attends a dinner party held by Ed's monied friends. Her feeling of displacement, which is compounded by being out of her class, is expressed through her memory of a picture "of a vase of flowers, impossible combinations. . . . The arrangement was beautiful, but it was something you could never see in real life" (213). Her belief that her alienation from her roots, her class, and her husband and children is decadent and corrupting is conveyed by her decision to climb into the Jacuzzi:

"It seemed too hot to bear, but she decided she would bear it—like a punishment, or an acquired taste that would turn delicious when she was used to it" (213).

Again in "Memphis," Mason traces a woman's desire for "freedom." Beverley reflects how, during the last months she lived with her former husband, "she had begun to feel that her mind was crammed with useless information, like a landfill, and there wasn't space deep down in her to move around in, to explore what was there. . . . She felt she had strong ideas and meaningful thoughts, but often when she tried to reach for one she couldn't find it. It was terrifying" (215). Her divorce does not seem to have brought her the increased autonomy she desired: she feels only "disembodied" and immobilized, as though she and her former husband are "stalled at a crossroads" (224). The story does, however, end with an increased sense of possibility as Beverley reflects: "Who knew what might happen or what anybody would decide to do on any given weekend or at any stage of life?" (232).

The final story, "Wish," takes a different perspective on change. It is told from the point-of-view of the eighty-three-year-old Sam, who is musing with his sister, Damson, on the past. Damson, who has never married, regrets her father's intervention in an early relationship and the subsequent death of her suitor, complaining that "'Pap ruined my life'" (237). Sam, however, is more acceptant of the events in his life. His wife, he believes, died "without needing him at all. And now he didn't need her" (241). His life now reduced mainly to his memories and "the small room where he had chosen to sleep," Sam realizes "he was happy." (241)

CHAPTER FIVE

Feather Crowns

Mason's most recent novel, *Feather Crowns* (1993), is a striking departure from her earlier fiction in that most of the narrative—which at nearly five hundred pages, is extensively elaborated—is set at the turn of the nineteenth and twentieth centuries. The novel is testimony to Mason's growing interest in local history since her return to live in Kentucky in 1990. She has explained that "The journey I've been on is a common enough one. First, you go out into the world in quest of understanding. Then you return to your origins and finally comprehend them."[1] Since the death of her father only months after her return to Kentucky,[2] Mason has explored her origins by informing herself about, and imagining, the lives of her forebears. In "The Way We Lived," for example, she recounts how her great-great-great-grandfather, Samuel Mason, was one of the pioneers of the Cumberland Settlements that "led to the founding of Nashville" and how two of his children "settled on Panther Creek, at Clear Springs, from whence all the relatives I have ever known sprang." A century later, in 1920, her grandfather moved eight miles away from Clear Springs to what became the Mason family farm.[3] The fiction writer's imagination fuses with the historian's investigative spirit as, in a recent article, Mason seeks to know "the mystery of my grandmother's mind." She describes how, after hearing reference to her grandmother's "depression" for the first time, after her death, she has sought to understand her grandmother's life and character. Mason recounts how her attempt to discover the history of her grandparents' lives disclosed family secrets shrouded in shame: through imaginative reconstruction she learned how her "grandmother spent the bloom of her youth dutifully caring for her father, who suffered from syphilis,"[4] and imagined how "the family's shame, although shrouded in silence, must have been stark and heavy."[5] Mason's quest to understand her grandmother's mind is, she believes, necessary to her understanding of herself: "My mind is hers, in part. Imagination connects me with her as surely as eye color and hair texture. I see myself in Granny's face."[6]

The genesis of *Feather Crowns* lies in a similar act of imaginative inquiry. The novel was inspired by an actual event: in 1896 Elizabeth Lyon gave birth to the first recorded quintuplets in the United States, "across the field" from where the Masons' farm now lies. Mason states: "For a brief time, they were world-famous, until curiosity-seekers handled the babies to death."[7] She has recalled that in *Feather Crowns,* "I had the nucleus of the plot—that's what I started with. But . . . where do you go with that? Here you have a woman who gives birth to quintuplets, and the world beats a path to her door. Well who is she? How does she feel about this? . . . You have to invent all this, you have to find it, and you have to make it come to life."[8] The narrative generated by Mason's attempt to imagine the thoughts and feelings of a woman who gave birth to quintuplets spans the years 1890–1963 and is told retrospectively from the point of view of Christianna ("Christie") Wheeler. It recounts her experience of pregnancy, parturition, nursing the infants, and their deaths. Mason traces Christie's reflections as she and her husband,

James, are then persuaded to travel around the South with the preserved bodies of the babies as an exhibit for the "edification" of the people.

Mason's account of the everyday life, albeit shaped by an extraordinary event, of a "country" woman and her extended family at the beginning of this century is a work of "historical realism."[9] She applies her keen eye for detail to the accurate representation of "events" that have gone largely unrecorded in official history as she explores the subjects of pregnancy, maternity, and feminine desire and friendship. Mason's evocation of a woman's story transects her elaboration of another narrative that has been marginalized by official history: that of the lives of farming people at a moment of social and economic transition. In her sustained attention to the details of her characters' lives, Mason invests her subjects with a significance rarely accorded them.[10] Her carefully historicized account of the life of her fictional character, Christianna Wheeler, brings to the foreground a strain of her work that has sometimes gone unrecognized in her depictions of contemporary life: her concern to give accurate "historical" representation of the intersection between the details of everyday life and the social and cultural forces that shape a particular moment. In *Feather Crowns* Mason combines an historian's retrospective analysis of these forces with the fiction writer's act of imaginative recreation. The effect of this is that she creates a feminine epic of the birth of modernity in the United States, unusually focused through the detailing of a woman's experience of giving birth and maternity. Realistic detail is held in equipoise with the symbolic significance of the narrative.

Here, as in her fiction set in the present, Mason pursues her interest in moments of historical transition. Moreover, as Harriet Pollack has noted, "as in her stories set in the late twentieth century, the novel charts historical change by looking at gender and sexual prescriptions and taboos in flux."[11] Mason's representation of the encroachments of modernity upon an isolated farming community near Hopewell, Kentucky, through her narrative of Christianna Wheeler's experiences, shows how the maternal body becomes the site upon which a battle between conflicting discourses is played out. New forms of knowledge compete with old and authority is relocated as people struggle to interpret and claim Christianna's experience for themselves. The novel, and its protagonist, bear witness to the onset of modernity through such trends as the decline of institutionalized religion in providing an authoritative interpretation of life's events and an accompanying movement from spiritual to secular interpretations of inner life[12]; the popularization of science as a legitimate source of knowledge, and, in particular, the increased authorization of the medical knowledge of the "expert," the doctor; changing conceptions of the "nation"; and the commercialization of everyday life that ushers in a culture of consumption.

In her representation of the cultural changes accompanying the shifts from an agrarian to a consumer-based economy, Mason identifies the seeds of many of the phenomena that characterize contemporary culture, as she depicts it elsewhere in her fiction.[13] Foremost among these shifts, as Mason presents them in *Feather Crowns,* is the emergence of "an age of spectacle."[14] In *Society of the Spectacle,* an analysis of the effects on society of mass consumption and communication at a later stage of capitalism (after the Second World War), Guy Debord has suggested that "the spectacle corresponds to the historical moment at which the commodity completes its colonization of social life"[15] and that "the spectacle is not a collection of images: rather, it is a social relationship between people that is mediated by images."[16] In *Feather Crowns* Mason depicts the beginnings of the process whereby labor becomes harnessed toward the production of commodities and the shift of social and economic relations to focus on the consumption of these commodities. The invasiveness of this process is symbolized by the commodification of Christie herself. Moreover, the novel shows how this economic shift produces a cultural shift, as the dissemination of "images" (at this moment, largely through advertising) is required to create a market for the commodities. Christie is invoked to offer such an "image," her maternity representing "reproduction, survival of the species, life and death, the body, sex and symbol,"[17] at a moment when the traditions that maintain a community, by enshrining through repetition a common response to these fundamental aspects of life, are being eroded.

As *Feather Crowns* shows, a significant aspect of the development of "an age of spectacle" is the production of the figure of the celebrity. Mason has said that the "big theme" of the novel is "American culture and the meaning of celebrity." She observes that people's hunger "to see anything grotesque" was "cruder then" and could be satisfied by "sideshows and carnival," but that it is a permutation of the same desire that now drives some people to tell "their innermost secrets" on television and others to consume them. Whereas before, people sought "external" manifestations of freakishness, she comments, "now we've gone inside, looking at people's minds to exploit them and invade their privacy, and people willingly co-operate in this."[18] In that celebrity is "the simultaneous evoking and annulling of mystery,"[19] Mason shows how Christianna Wheeler is displayed both to embody passing ways of life and "mysterious" bodily and sexual excesses and to show how, through the "enlightenment" of modernity, such "primitive" mysteries can be dispelled.

At the center of the processes of modernization that Mason represents in *Feather Crowns* is the objectification of the female body, and specifically the maternal body. Through the spectacular display of Christianna Wheeler and her babies, a grotesque dissolution of the boundaries between the public and the private commences. A further thematic continuity between this novel and Mason's previous works occurs as she connects the public desire to consume this spectacle, specifically of a mother and her pain, to a people mourning both personal losses and cultural losses relating to the erosion of values associated with a traditional concept of community. Just as the public present their grief to the exhibited Christianna, much later in the century people will seek to assuage their personal and "national" losses with spectacles presented on television, as Mason has shown in *In Country*.

The novel comprises seven parts, the first five of which present Christie's memories of the personal history surrounding the birth and death of the quintuplets. Mason's closely detailed and realistic account of these events immerses the reader in the minutiae of a woman's experience of maternity, while also situating the maternal body as symbolically central to the large cultural changes introduced by modernity. This focus upon the maternal body, which balances realism with symbolism, is established in the novel's memorable opening paragraph: "Christianna Wheeler, big as a washtub and confined to bed all winter with the heaviness of her unusual pregnancy, heard the midnight train whistling up from Memphis. James was out there somewhere. He would have to halt the horse and wait in the darkness for the hazy lights of the passenger cars to jerk past, before he could fly across the track and up the road toward town. He was riding his Uncle Wad's horse, Dark-Fire."[20] Here femininity is equivalent to interiority, privacy, and domestic space, the desire to escape from which is one of the themes of *In Country*. These lines immediately evoke Christie's feeling of incarceration within both her body and the domestic interior from which she will seek to flee after the death of her babies. Her entrapment within a cumbersome body is lightly contrasted with her husband's relative freedom, on horseback. This freedom is compromised, however, by the fact that the horse is owned by his uncle Wad. In addition, Christie's immobility contrasts with the movement of the train, which is to accrue various metaphoric connotations each time she notices its passage. Above all, it is the herald of modernity, signifying the compression of time and distance and the encroachment of industrialization upon rural life, which modern technology will bring. This process, as depicted by the novel, will include the erosion of the Wheelers' livelihood, cultivating the "dark-fire" tobacco crop. Mason recounts how, "as manufactured cigarettes grew more popular, the dark leaf lost its value. It was almost worthless under the tobacco trust, and farmers tried to withhold their crops from the market." Some farmers mobilized against the trust, forcing others to join their association. The conflict escalated into "the Black Patch Wars . . . a bloody, awful thing spreading all over that country" (424). As Mason will show, the "progress" of modernization is double-edged: James's need for the light cast by the train to penetrate the darkness that envelops him anticipates the electric lights of modernity that will hold him and Christie in their glare for the "enlightenment" of the public.

Christie's ambivalence toward the cultural changes that engulf her is symbolized by the ambiguous connotations of the train: while it brings the destruction of her privacy, which contributes to the estrangement between her and James, it will also promise new freedom when it transports her away from the farm. Moreover, Christie frequently associates the train with sexual desire, imagining, for example, her love-making with James as their being "on the train, riding the locomotive, charging wildly into the night," (7) and recalling how "a sudden passion gripped them . . . and the train whistle sounded, merging with the long, slow release of desire" (59).

As she lies in her confinement, fearing that she is about to give birth to "unnatural" progeny, Christie seeks to understand the desire that led to their conception. Mason locates feminine desire, for both sexual and other forms of self-expression, at the center of her text, and yet no amenable discourse is available to Christie through which to articulate it. She recalls how, on her wedding night, "the mystery of how the man connected with the woman and planted his seed was something that had never been explained" (49) and refers to sexual intercourse as "the part nobody ever talked about" (47). She surmises that she "knew now why women wouldn't speak of it to each other—admitting the pleasure would be too embarrassing" (50). The dominant cultural discourse about sexuality, that of Christianity, informs her that "it was shameful to enjoy it. It was sinful if you weren't married. There were words for that in the Bible: fornication, whoring" (42). Christie internalizes this discourse, believing that "the monster inside her" (32) has been produced by an "excess of loving" (57) that was "shameless" and "sinful."

Troubled by the "monstrous" progeny she is carrying, Christie associates her own desire with a public event in which she recognizes the mobilization of a similarly "excessive," and transgressive, desire. She recalls how, early in her pregnancy, she attended an evangelical camp meeting at Reelfoot lake with her sister-in-law, Amanda Wheeler. There, the preachers whipped up the crowds with prognostications of a millennial apocalypse in the form of an impending earthquake that would wreak divine retribution for the "sickness . . . all over the land" (75). The "new age," they foretold, "would bring evils and wonders in equal proportion" (65). The response of the onlookers to the preachers' injunctions to repent of their sin and seek forgiveness before the imminent Judgment Day was one of ecstatic release. Amanda, for example, fell to the ground in "abandon," and Christie noticed a woman nursing her baby "in front of everybody" (80). Christie reflects that "she always loved the spectacle of a camp meeting," (64) but this form of "spectacle" still has a carnivalesque quality, whereby people can participate to transgress temporarily the boundaries of their "proper" roles before resuming them in their everyday life. This contrasts with the spectacle that is later to subsume Christie, where she will required to remain frozen in her role as icon. As she listens to

Brother Cornett, she feels that his "energetic performance had touched something in her that had been all knotted up, and now it seemed to be coming unraveled. She had felt this once before, when a fever broke" (76). She interprets this response as a sexual attraction to Brother Cornett, which subsequently contributes to the guilt she feels for the "monstrousness" of the progeny she is carrying. Christie's identification of her desire and the conception of her babies with the prophecies of millennial signs and wonders will be echoed by the public nomination of her babies as "a wonder of the world," which invokes her body and its offspring as a symbol of the spirit of the age.

The desire that Christie retrospectively places at the center of her history is an expression of her wish for agency, which will later take other forms, although even at this point she is aware that "in those first years of her marriage," she "felt simultaneously giddy and ecstatic, mentally agitated and surging with fire and ambition" (48). Christie's desire expresses her will to be a subject who can act upon her own volition, but from Mason's opening depiction of Christie's confinement to childbed, she shows how many of the forces of modernity conspire to objectify her.

As the train from Memphis passes, Christie is surrounded by the community of women who traditionally would help her give birth. Mason does not depict the counsel of these women as unequivocally helpful: Christie's mother has told her that "if a woman couldn't nurse her babies, they would never grow up to mind her" (94), and Christie is terrified by her Aunt Sophie's embittered warning that "'it's nine months from the marriage bed to the death bed'" (7). Christie and the other women do, nevertheless, place their trust in the traditional birthing techniques of the midwife, Hattie Hurt. The advent of medical science is signified, however, by the arrival of Dr. Foote to deliver the babies, against the will of the women, who ask him "'ain't this women's work?'" (27). Christie has already encountered Foote, whose examination of her body she found to be an unwonted invasion of her privacy, despite his pinning up her dress as "a barrier that kept them from seeing each other's faces" (19). As Harriet Pollack has remarked, "This barrier does not obscure the uneasy medical violation of a culturally normative sexual separation—a separation strong enough to prevent Christie from telling James about even the babies' kicking."[21]

Christie ponders on the nature of "the man who made it his business to care for other people's bodies. How could a person do that? To touch a stranger's body, to take authority over it—it would require either courage or cruelty. The preachers cared for the soul, and the doctors took ahold of the body" (88). Her realization that the doctor's claiming of authority over her requires the objectification of her body is borne out when Foote rearranges her, to her discomfort, in preparation for the birth: her sister-in-law, Alma, remarks: "You better get her up and bend her over," to which Foote responds: "No, I can work better with her in this position" (28). The objectifying propensities of medical science are compounded when Foote tells Christie he has invited his friend to visit her: "Dr. Cooley won't charge. He just wants a look, out of scientific interest" (112).

When Christie gives birth to the quintuplets (a term she first encounters in the report of the event in the local newspaper), the townspeople claim her as a local celebrity, declaring her to be

"Hopewell's Mother of the Year" and the Wheelers "First Family of our City" (149). Visits from neighbors and townspeople are soon encompassed by the arrival of strangers. Christie reflects that "something happened that . . . was the turning point of her life" when "the 3.03 train from Memphis," ironically named "the Friendship," stopped to disgorge its passengers across the cornfield and into her home. These passengers, some of whom are returning from a visit to the Memphis Exposition with its "displays of every kind of wonder pertaining to science and industry" (206), desire to witness another "wonder" of the modern age. Mason's descriptions of the seething crowds of strangers who invade Christie's home, ignoring all boundaries between public and private space, vividly evokes modernity's colonization of previously sacrosanct personal and familial spaces. This is epitomized by the man who, finding no other means of access, climbs in though the window of her front room. Elevated to a celebrity, Christie is violated by the public gaze. She lies watching "the people pass through her house in a bewildering tide of laughing, crying, snorts, and high-pitched spurts, whistles, squeals, barks, mews, and shouts—a babble of baby talk" (180). She tries to protect herself and the babies she is nursing from their view, but she feels "naked, like a plucked chicken" (166).

A report in a St. Louis newspaper, which refers to her and James as "'a simple country woman and her yeoman farmer husband'" who live in "'a humble three-room abode'" (151), reveals to her how she is perceived by these strangers. Christie realizes that the farm and her home, as well as she and her husband, represent a "simple" rural way of life, already associated with the past, to her urban visitors. This characterization undermines her sense of the value of both herself and her home. If the crowd of strangers seems animal-like to Christie, she also internalizes the perception of herself implied in Wad's comment that "'she done dropped a litter, like a sow and a gang of little pigs" (35). Her surroundings now seem "suffused with smells of cooking and babies and close human habitation" (166). Whereas she had previously taken pride in the furniture that James had made for them to begin their married life together, she has heard one of the strangers describe it as "right tacky," (199) and looking at her home, full of strangers, she feels "ashamed," noticing that "the wallpaper, though new, looked suddenly shabby, the handmade furniture too modest, the place too small" (166). A small palliative to this alteration of her sense of value is offered by the woman who observes to her that "'this room is so personal. . . . What you have here, with your family, money could never buy'" (202). Through Mason's evocation of the strangers' perceptions of Christie's class, as defined by her means and taste, and Christie's internalization of these perceptions, Mason poignantly depicts the emotional cost of Christie's growing awareness of class differences. The adjustment of self-perception that this requires Christie to make anticipates the effects of repositioning through a shift in the class structure later in the twentieth century, upon which Mason has commented: "the shift from the independence of rural life is a profound upheaval. . . . People are being redefined as working class, which is a reduction in status, for the yeoman farmer was his own boss."[22]

The strangers' view of Christie and her home marks the beginning of an irreversible process of the commodification of her everyday life. This is quickly capitalized upon by Wad, who decides to charge entry to see Christie and "THE AMAZING 5 BABIES" (179). Christie, hearing Wad's proposition, "felt peculiar, as she always did when she overheard men talking business. This time, she was the business" (172). The discourse of commercialization casts Christie as an object of both transaction and consumption. This process is compounded by the commercialization of motherhood, which occurs as various firms use her to advertise their products: "Howell's Drugs and Sundries," for example, send her "Fortune Nursing Bottles" and "store-bought diapers," offering "to be of service in supplying all your baby needs" (125). The commercial value placed on these artifacts contrasts with the sentimental value Christie has formerly placed on natural objects, such as the gifts James gave her when they were "courting." The process of commercialization is accelerated by the development of various forms of communications technology, as is exemplified by the telegram Christie receives from the *Louisville Courier-Journal,* the photographs that are taken of her, and the imminent arrival of telephones in Hopewell.

The commercialization of all areas of life is further evinced to Christie upon the death of her babies. James places the corpse of Minnie, the first child to die, in the springhouse, to preserve it until he can bury it. The traditional rites of death are communal: women would tend the body, and the family would keep a vigil with the body. Christie's father tells her that he "could have cut one [a casket] out of pine. I could have made ye some nice brass handles," and her mother "would have lined the inside with some bleached domestic and trimmed it on the outside with balls of fringe held down by leaden rose-beaded tacks" (261). However, due to the advertisement of his trade they will bring, Christie and James are offered the services of Mr. Mullins, the proprietor of "one of those newfangled funeral parlors" who is "versed in the skills of sympathy" (223). Mullins informs them that there are "remarkable techniques" that will enable him to preserve the bodies, and they are duly placed on display in a glass case in his funeral parlor. The commodification of her now preserved babies seems to Christie to be complete, as they appear "no longer . . . her flesh and blood. They were objects, painted pink . . . fine handiwork" (259).

Christie watches from behind a curtain as townspeople and strangers from further afield file through Mullins's "Slumber Room," and she realizes that "people still wanted to say they had seen the babies—dead or alive, it seemed not to matter" (200). From the time when crowds filled her home to observe her still-living babies, Christie had realized that here is a connection between the public's desire for spectacle and death. As the strangers stared at her and the babies in her home, "for a moment she felt as though she were in her own coffin. It was her funeral and the people were filing past. But instead of weeping over her body, they were marveling over what her body had produced" (198). Christie senses how the subject of the spectacle is metaphorically deprived of life by its viewers' objectifying gaze, a process that has become horribly literal when the onlookers view her preserved babies.

Central to Christie's story, however, is the fact that her own desires militate against the public's attempt to lock her in its gaze. From the outset she is ambivalent about her role as the object of the public gaze: while she resents the invasion of her privacy, she also feels proud that the birth of the quintuplets has made her "extraordinary." As she lay imprisoned in the gaze of the crowd, "she was glowing inside, as if her soul had escaped her body and traveled to some busy scene in a stranger's house, maybe in another country" (198). In addition, as the strangers view her, she is also watching them: "She wasn't the show—she was watching the show" (180). Christie is the onlooker again as she watches the crowds from behind the curtain in Mullins's funeral parlor.

As she mourns, Christie's sense of a self, separate from the babies and the spectacle within which they have all been confined, begins to crystallize again. It is Mullins's exclusion of Mittens Dowdy from the funeral parlor that incites her to feel "the clarity of anger for the first time since she lost the babies" (263). Unable to provide enough milk for all the babies, Christie had accepted the services of a wet nurse, the black Mittens Dowdy. Although to some extent bound by the racial prejudices of her class, her friendship with Mittens gradually sensitizes Christie to racial injustice. Harriet Pollack has observed that "Christie is receptive to an education in racial hierarchy in part because she has already felt class hierarchy," as is evinced by "her thoughts about Mrs. Blankenship."[23] When Mrs. Blankenship, the wife of the planing-mill owner to whom James is in debt, condescends to visit Christie in childbed, Christie is oppressed by her memories of the woman reviving her when she fainted during her pregnancy: Mrs. Blankenship's "silky voice" and evident wealth made "Christie's own need for a new work dress . . . feel shabby" (144). Christie's contact with Mittens

Dowdy prompts her to reflect anew, for example, on an incident in her childhood. Uncle Obie, who did odd jobs for her family and "loved snakes," was avoided by some people "since a person without fear of snakes was said to have the Devil in him." At this point in Christie's education in an awareness of social injustice, it is the fact that she thinks about Uncle Obie that is significant, as she is not yet ready to question the manner of his death: "Christie remembered little about him but knew he had been found dead along a rutted road one chilly morning. People said a whip snake had come along and thrashed him to death" (118). Increasingly attuned to social inequality, therefore, Christie is prompted to act by Mullins's exclusion of Mittens Dowdy, taking her into the forbidden precincts of the funeral parlor to pay her respects to the babies.

During the summer of 1900, while her babies lie preserved in Mullins's funeral parlor, Christie goes through the first phases of grieving, which she finds embrace a surprising variety of emotions. She has been the subject of town gossip because she did not cry much at the funeral, but, she reflects: "her grief was too deep. And it was hidden under the strange exhilaration she often felt" (258). During this time, when she and James are unable to communicate their grief to each other, her estrangement from her husband begins: planting corn together, "they worked silently, as if they were both afraid their grief would come pouring out and flood the field" (267). Christie finds some consolation, however, in reclaiming her "self," as, for example, when she sees a fox, which she would normally fear. On this occasion, she decides to approach the animal with "an unaccustomed boldness," feeling a longing "to touch him." Her moment alone with the fox is disturbed by Wad, who exclaims "'If I'd had my gun I'd 'a' got him'" (266).

In this mood of yearning restlessness, of a grieving wherein she feels at once "empty with sorrow" and "so keenly alive that every speck of creation jumped out at her with a brilliant vividness" (270), Christie receives Greenberry McCain's proposition that she and James accompany the babies on "the Fair Day Exhibition Series, an educational series of lectures and diversions, for the purpose of educating the generally curious and concerned public about the Hopewell Quintuplets" (303). Christie and James are persuaded that this is an opportunity to pay back their debt to Wad Wheeler, but more significantly, Christie intends to use it to express her anger to the public whose handling of the babies she believes caused their deaths: "she had an urgent purpose—to get out there and face the public, to show them her pain. She wanted to get revenge on them, on people she didn't even know" (320). Her display of anger, she believes, would make her "master of the scene," so that the people "would slink off, carrying her sickness away from her" (312). The tour also promises her temporary freedom from her "shallow roots" (311) on the Wheelers' farm, and she feels "ready to confront the world, with all her anger and curiosity and urgency" (314).

Christie and James leave Hopewell on the train, preparing to become modern subjects themselves, as they see "the view all those travelers had had" (319). But in Greenberry's traveling show, they and their babies are positioned once again as a spectacle for the consumption and "enlightenment of the general public" (328). As the show moves from the Nashville Opera House to the less elevated agricultural fairs, Christie realizes that they are being displayed as grotesques, along with other "curiosities" such as "the Snake Woman from Borneo" and the hermaphrodite, "Charley Lou Pickles." Christie has not anticipated, however, that people would approach her as *mater dolorosa,* the spectacle of a bereaved mother who, in her suffering, would understand their own losses: "she hadn't expected so many people to bring their own grief to her. . . . Just yesterday, a woman gave her a likeness of a little girl with curled hair and a large hair bow, lying with her doll on a bed. The woman's sorrow crashed into Christie's own like trains head on. Christie had no words to offer the woman. She didn't know what solace the sight of the five lifeless babies could give. Could her babies' deaths really have been a greater gift to the world than their lives might have been?" (336). In the spectacle of bereavement that Christie presents, the people find a mute symbol of their own suffering.

However, while her public role is as a symbolic object, Christie's narrative traces the awakening of her own critical and compassionate consciousness and how she finds a voice and a language through which to articulate her story. Christie's desire to observe as well as to be observed sustains her on Greenberry's tour. Her consciousness of racial inequality heightened by her recognition of prejudice against Mittens, she is a keen observer of the postbellum South across which the entourage is traveling. She notices that "the effects of the War were everywhere," remarking on "the defeated faces of the people" (340). Gazing across the cotton fields where "Negroes" work, she feels "she had never seen such desolation" (341). As she travels, Christie increasingly develops a voice and a will to articulate her observations. Back in the Wheeler household, little time or value has been accorded to the expression of emotion: as Alma tells her after the death of her babies, "'there ain't no time to set around for sorrow'" (255). Christie begins to protest against this silencing, and the masculine regime it supports. For example, when her rather meek brother-in-law, Boone, assures her that she has to go on McCain's tour "on account of the tobaccer," Christie corrects him: "'No, we *don't* have to . . . I said I *wanted* to go. *I'm* the one that decided," a point she reiterates when Boone fails to hear her assertion of volition (304). She asserts her view again, perhaps unheard, as the crowds look at her preserved babies: "'My babies was wooled to death. . . . By people just like you'" (328). Early on the tour, she finds a public voice when she writes a letter documenting her observations to the *Hopewell Chronicle.* Although her voice is constrained by her "attempting the voice of small-town journalistic decorum and 'trying for high tone,'"[24] she records her observations with an historian's eye for significant detail and ignores James's warning that "'they might not print that part about niggers'" (335).

With this developing social and self-awareness, Christie's resistance against her subjection is precipitated by her anger when the "wagon-show" of which she forms a part is staged to coincide with a public hanging in Birmingham, Alabama. This "coincidence," she suspects, is "so the weekend could be a holiday festival, with increased profits" (388). While consciously decrying this exploitation of herself, Christie is also resisting a construction of herself that she has not yet fully articulated. Earlier, when Christie watched the members of the public in Mullins's funeral parlor "wanting to see the babies through their

curious eyes," she had presciently sensed that "she was on display then, too, like a criminal waiting to be hanged" (261).
Jacqueline Rose, in "The Cult of Celebrity," has referred to the
"passion and loathing . . . of celebrity," speculating that there is
"something murderous in our relation to celebrity."[25] She connects this both to the "violence" that "public curiosity" wreaks
upon its object, whose "mystery" it wishes to master, and to the
ambiguous function that the celebrity may be asked to perform.
The celebrity figure is often required to demonstrate the existence of an "ostentatious morality," but this might be by virtue of
the celebrity's transgression of that morality. Rose asks: "Could
it be then that celebrity is indeed our guilty secret, a veiled way
of putting into public circulation certain things which do not easily admit of public acknowledgment?" If this is the case, then the
condition of celebrity becomes "a ritual of public humiliation,"
the celebrity figure providing the scapegoat for "shame, or shaming."[26]

In Christie's case, as an icon of fecund motherhood, desig-
nated "Hopewell's Mother of the Year" and member of "First
Family of our city"(149), she has been asked to symbolize the
survival and flowering of a community and its values at a time
when rapid change is irrevocably altering that community. At the
same time, the excessive number of her progeny suggests that
she has in some way transgressed those values, and the element
of "shaming" in the display of her and the dead babies as
grotesques is in part a punishment of her. Christie's compliance
with this "punishment" is ambivalent, however. Rose, referring
to the ambivalence of celebrity figures toward their own status,
has observed that "public celebrity might be an elaborate diver-

sion from the complex, often punitive audience, inside the mind."[27] At a moment of widespread transition from religious to secular values, Christie, who has often configured as "sinful" what she has regarded as bodily, sexual, and emotional excess, has at some level embraced her "shame." Her refusal to be displayed concurrently with the public hanging therefore marks her rejection of both the public's desire to cast her as a scapegoat and her own assumption of guilt. This recognition, which is to some extent shared by James in his anger at the planned event, advances their mourning. They share a moment of physical intimacy, rare since their bereavement. Grief and pleasure mingle as they weep for their "lost innocence," and they decide to leave the tour.

Christie proposes that they deposit the babies with Dr. Johnson at the Institute of Man, Washington, an institute "that studies scientific curiosities," and that, Johnson claims, "is devoted to the advancement of science, not to public entertainment" (330). Despite her treatment at the hands of Dr. Foote and McCain, supposed representatives of medical science and the education of the public, Christie's decision is in keeping with the development of her character throughout the narrative. In this respect, she is a figure of modernity, as well as having been exploited by its putative proponents. Throughout her experiences, Christie has been sustained by an inquiring mind that remains alive to occurrences in both the natural and the social worlds.

Early on, she recalls how, unlike other girls, she stayed on at school beyond the twelfth grade, avidly pursuing her interest in local history. The main source of "knowledge" available to

Christie upon her entry into the Wheeler household, however, is the folk wisdom of the other women. Amanda, for example, reads the signs of persimmon seeds and places an ax under Christie's bed "to cut the pain" of childbirth. Christie is "intrigued" to notice that Amanda and Mittens Dowdy share this superstitious approach to the world, sharing "many of the same notions about bad luck and signs" (119). This is one of several common properties Christie observes between members of the marginalized communities of women and African Americans. This attempt of the disempowered to "read" the world is strikingly exemplified when Amanda's daughter, Little Bunch, who suffers from fits, finds two "feather crowns" in the bolster on Christie's bed. The women offer various interpretations of these "signs": "If they were in a person's pillow, it was a sign the person was going to die, Mama said. But Amanda had told Christie that when a crown was found after death, it meant the person had gone to Heaven" (271). The women's search for meaning in signs is connected to a more authoritative cultural tradition when Amanda and Christie attend the camp meeting at Reelfoot, where the Christian tradition of searching for the revelation of divine meaning in natural phenomena culminates in the preachers' apocalyptic discourse of "signs and wonders." This is a tradition that Christie herself has inherited, through her descent from her great-grandfather, "who had become a Methodist minister late in life" (66).[28] Against this translation of natural phenomena into "signs," however, Christie has both a discerning aesthetic appreciation of the details of the natural world and a desire for "factual" information that will explain it. As she looks out over the local landscape, she realizes she has "an outlook, something directing her eyes so that they didn't miss anything," (252) and she knows that James cannot see the beauty of the tobacco fields "the way she did, his mind was so full of what had to be done" (292). The legacy of her Christian faith remains in her belief that the birth of the quintuplets "must be a token of some kind" (268), and yet she tells James that "everything is a question" (269). At the conclusion of her narrative, Christie speaks of her "loss of faith," which, as Harriet Pollack has observed, "covers a complexity of change," including "loss of faith in formal religion" and "finally loss of faith in 'God's mysterious ways' and in God Himself."[29] As she turns from religious faith to science to seek the answers to her questions, Christie adumbrates the movement of modernity.

On McCain's tour, she turns for information to *The Encyclopedia of Animal Life,* where she reads "all about the science of life," but when she tries to explain her interest about "slipper animalcule, or paramecium" to James, he asks if she is "losing her mind." Christie's desire to make "a contribution to knowledge. And history" (411) impels her to donate the babies to the Institute of Man. She welcomes Johnson's courteous treatment of them, which contrasts with McCain's inconsiderateness, and she respects Johnson's profession that "we collect unusual medical phenomena" such as "President Lincoln's bloodstains . . . the preserved bodies of several pairs of Siamese twins . . . the organs of a number of hermaphrodites" for "study" rather than "to put our collection on display like a lurid sideshow" (411). Mason's representation of Johnson is ambiguous, nevertheless. He invites Christie to recount her experiences to illuminate her question of "why *does* such a thing happen?" (411), but when she tries to explain how "'they got me all riled up. It was the Wheelers. The Wheeler clan" (412), which she believes "'was her own story, what she'd kept to herself'" (413), Johnson stops writing. As he has explained, "'we're only concerned with the natural phenomenon itself. . . . We're not after the social history'" (409). It is the "social history" that Christie seeks to explain in her narrative, as she realizes that the question "wasn't *why* it happened—that couldn't be known; it was what the world made of it that was at issue" (417).

In the concluding two parts of the novel, Christie offers a retrospective account of the "social history" that will interpret her personal history. The first of these accounts is prompted by a conversation with a young woman whom Christie meets on a train in 1937, when she is traveling to see the Dionne quintuplets in Canada. Her final account is delivered into a tape recorder at the behest of her granddaughter after Christie's ninetieth birthday has occasioned the citizens of Hopewell to reclaim her as a local celebrity. This account is offered in 1963, on the eve of the emergence of the second wave of feminism in the United States. Christie's retrospective analysis of the forces that have most closely shaped her life anticipates the concerns of that movement, although it will arrive too late to deliver her the freedoms she has sought.

Much of Christie's narrative has focused upon maternity and bereavement, as she has experienced them as an object of the public gaze, transected by the forces of modernity. However, other narrative strands are interwoven with this, through which Christie delineates relations between the members of the extended family of Wheelers. These strands provide a powerful commentary on the position of women of Christie's class, particularly as this was determined by expectations of their role within the family, at the end of the nineteenth century through the opening decades of the twentieth century. Christie's communication of her story to her modern granddaughter conveys the continued relevance of her observations to contemporary women and men. As Sarah Wood has commented, "*Feather Crowns* is about ethics and whether the family or the mass of opinion has the right to determine the future of any individual, particularly children."[30]

In much of the early part of her narrative, Christie situates her relationship with her husband as central to her personal history, but as the narrative proceeds, she attributes increasing significance to other relationships. Christie's portrayal of her relationship with James is attuned to the difficulties created by unequal gender roles and expectations, as for example, when she is dismayed by James's endorsement of Wad's authority over the household, or when her "bitterness" at James's exercise of his own authority over her "drove deep in her, into a place where she saved such emotions, a place where they could grow into something useful" (258). On the tour she feels distanced from James by his passivity at the hands of McCain, but she also understands that removing James from his work on the farm has divested him of his sense of purpose and volition. Sarah Wood has commented that the novel reveals "the difficulty of being left without your traditional understanding,"[31] and it is partly this difficulty that undermines the Wheelers' marriage. Christie recalls with a distanced sadness that "of course James died in the middle of his work" (453).

Retrospectively, Christie recognizes the importance of female friendships to her. Her closest alliances are with Alma and Amanda Wheeler. In Alma, Christie finds a proponent of the Wheeler ethos of hard work and little communication. Alma efficiently attends to Christie's needs in childbirth but does not believe Christie should prolong the process of mourning. When she tries to bring this to a close by taking Christie to see the babies at Mullins's funeral parlor, Christie resists the authority Alma has assumed over her: "She wouldn't let Alma tell her what to do, or what to believe, or what to feel. She didn't want Alma to intrude on her specialness or have anything to do with lifting the blame [she] pulled over herself like a heavy quilt" (283). When Alma's husband, Thomas Hunt, disappears, Alma shows no sense of loss, and his name is omitted from her tombstone.

Amanda, however, is a figure who haunts Christie's narrative with her unfulfilled longing. Christie recalls Amanda's fragility among the practical Wheelers, likening her to "a rose blooming in a tobacco patch" (55). This simile is compounded by a second memory, where Christie recollects how "Wad spit tobacco juice onto a hollyhock Amanda had trained up the drainpipe near the back door. The juice stained the bottom blossom" (55–6). Amanda presents Christie with a mirror of her own desires to some extent, but in Amanda's yearning Christie perceives an instability with which she refuses to identify. Even though Christie is aware that Amanda's need, like her own, is for more than sex, Christie associates the "hidden," "dangerous," and "unthinkable" trait of Amanda's personality with sexual desire. She recalls how, at Reelfoot, where Amanda fell over in ecstatic "abandon," her "shirtwaist was spotted with sweat stains" (106) and how she disturbed Amanda, in disarray, with Thomas Hunt in the smokehouse. Despite her own sense of shame, Christie tries to dissociate herself from any identification with Amanda's disruptive desire: " she couldn't keep up with what went on in the smokehouse. . . . Her own sins were more than she could face" (243). Whereas Christie's narrative reveals her developing understanding of the forces that have shaped her position as a woman, Amanda, as Harriet Pollack notes, "can neither fit nor successfully break with the social prescription for gendered selflessness. She is an ancestor of those Mason women who will escape 'proper' gender behaviors, but she lives before their time.'"[32]

Lacking a discourse through which to interpret her position, or an adequate means with which to change it, Amanda seeks in Christie an ally against the family into which they have married. Her appeal to Christie's friendship is based partly on what she perceives as their common suffering, but just as Christie feels helpless in her role as *mater dolorosa,* receptacle of the people's grief, so she is uneasy with Amanda's gestures of sympathetic identification with her loss. She is disturbed by a letter from Amanda in which "her grief seemed like an offering of friendship'" (373) and by Amanda's gift of a "small wreath made out of human hair," which includes locks she had taken from the babies. To Christie, "the overall effect was of a carefully preserved bouquet of garden posies—sun-faded and drenched of their color. Dead" (423). Harriet Pollack has noted that the wreath is "full of labor and even love, but without the capacity to transform."[33] As such, it expresses Amanda's inability to move beyond the pain and loss that inform her longing. Christie recalls how Amanda's loneliness was deepened after Little Bunch's death and how a second scene occurred in the smokehouse: Amanda's suicide. With hindsight, Christie reflects that "It's the only way [Amanda] can say 'I'm free.' That's what Mandy was a-saying when she strung herself up" (453).

Christie's own experience of pain and the attempt to understand grief is central to her account of her life, and early in her mourning she reasons that life is a series of losses, each of which prepares one to experience the next more acutely, "as if life were a simple circle, with events occurring and recurring, and when you encountered an event the second time you had learned to feel its pain" (263). But through her narrative, Christie attempts to break this cycle of repetition, transforming the potential of events to cause her pain, through an understanding of them. Christie is aided in this attempt by her friendships with Mittens Dowdy and the Wiggins sisters, three women whom she meets "at a cotton festival in Little Rock," where they are singing and she is being exhibited with her babies. While her recognition of their common suffering is an element of these friendships, the women's "capacity to transform" pain, as is expressed in their songs, which "punctuate Christie's education,"[34] inspires Christie. In the melody Mittens sings as she feeds Christie's babies, "as if she were passing secrets on to the babies," (120) and the Wiggins sisters' songs, which drift through Christie's tent "like sweet cooking smells," (361) suffering is transformed into knowledge and an embrace of life. It is both Christie's understanding of suffering, particularly as it is connected to social injustice, and her respect for those who have transcended it that render her receptive to the song she hears one day when she is enjoying a moment of freedom on her tour, having strayed alone along a riverside path in Vicksburg. The song is recognizable to her as being "like a Negro sundown holler—that long, loud collective sigh of relief she had been hearing every night when the field workers quit" (374). Entranced by its power and beauty, which remind her of Mittens' songs, she follows the sound to its source. There, a man is singing about "a large woman in a house by the cotton fields, where he worked" (374), and Christie can "almost visualize that immense, dark woman coming to the singer at night, giving him the strength to get through the day's labor" (376). The song both arouses in Christie "a longing for something new and surprising," which is how she now interprets the "excessive desire" she felt at Reelfoot, and seems to articulate "her own accumulated rage and sorrow, coming out in deep, clear notes" (375). The effect of the song is to focus her grief, "reorganizing her memories, sharpening them and shaping them for some new purpose" (375). The song stimulates an epiphany for Christie, enabling her to interpret her grief more clearly: after hearing it, she "felt she had turned a corner into brilliant sunshine" (378).

The concluding two parts of the novel present Christie's "reorganization" of her memories. Her reflections offer a sharp critique of the constraints that her extended family placed upon her. During the "hard" years following her return to the farm after McCain's tour, Christie's assertions of independence, through her visits to Mittens for instance, convinced Wad that she was "plumb crazy," and she surmises that Wad and Alma even considered sending her to an asylum. Her indictment of family life, as she has experienced it, is absolute: she tells her granddaughter "the truth about people, how they'll just eat you alive. And families can smother you" (447). Despite her memories of the ways in which the arrival of modernity violated her, she also recognizes the freedoms it promised and has no nostalgia for the close bonds of a tight-knit rural community. She explains: "I was looking for something. I wanted the free and unattached generousness of a stranger meeting a stranger, where nothing familiar can cast a shadow of obligation on you, or a mirror reflection. No influences, no judgments. . . . I wanted to explore the whole world. I wanted to know others" (447). She reminds her granddaughter that "women didn't get to do things back then like they can now" and acknowledges, with hindsight, that "we went traipsing around that fall because I wanted more of it. I wanted to get away from the farm and see what was out there in the wide blue world" (447).

Christie perspicaciously extends her critique of "the family" to "the nation," discerning how she was invoked to symbolize the connection between them. The South she surveyed on McCain's tour in 1900 was still recovering from the effects of the Civil War, and it was against this backdrop that, both locally and across the South, she was conjured as a symbol of restored civic pride (as Wad Wheeler put it, "'you've done the beatin'est thing to hit this country since President Jackson bought it from the Indians'" [36]) and national progress. Retrospectively in 1937, Christie rejects this concept of the nation. Her reflection on the death of her son in France in the First World War anticipates Samantha Hughes's contestation of the grounds of patriotism in *In Country,* set nearly fifty years later: although "she was told she gave him for her country," "any mother would rather have her boy than any country in the world. . . . A person could sacrifice all she held dear for a land that didn't return the favor" (425). She recalls the invasion of her home by the crowds, who sought in the figure of motherhood and home she presented in her "humble abode" a symbol of a familial and communal unity, which was already being erased by the processes of industrialization and modernization. She observes: "I believe they just thought the whole nation was one big family. . . . I knew how cruel a big family could be" (451).

In her final retrospective, Christie is skeptical, therefore, about the idealization of past rural families and communities, particularly on the grounds of the gender roles and relations they embodied. Looking back on her life, "she could see a string of pies—pies at funerals and pies at weddings and pies at birthings. The rhythm of eating something special carried people in and out of life. She saw the women waiting on the men and the sick and the old and the young. The women were constantly in motion" (426). Her perception of modernity is more ambivalent: her critique of the invasiveness of "the age of spectacle" is balanced against what she regards as the positive changes that modernity introduced, such as new ways of understanding the world and, particularly, the liberation of women from constricting gender roles. Her final words are an affirmation of life—the kind of affirmation she respected in Mittens and the Wiggins sisters. What she affirms, however, are not the sophisticated pleasures that modernity has brought, but the small, "natural" pleasures gleaned from her life on the farm: "I want to watch the sun come up and hear a hen cackle over a new-laid egg and feel a kitten purr. And I want to see a flock of blackbirds whirl over the field, making music. Things like that are absolutely new ever time they happen" (454). It is these pleasures that Mason's contemporary characters struggle to retain, separated as they have become from the natural world by the advancements of modernity.

NOTES

Chapter One: Background and Biography

1. "Bobbie Ann Mason," *Signature,* Program 101, dir. Marsha Cooper Hellard, prod. Guy Mendes, videotape ed. James Walker, narr. Marsha Cooper Hellard, the Kentucky Network, Lexington, 1995.

2. "Bobbie Ann Mason," in *Current Biography Yearbook,* 1989, ed. Charles Moritz et al. (New York: H.W. Wilson, 1989), 388–89. Culture shock is a recurring concern of Mason's nonfiction as well as her fiction. See, for example, her article "Kath Walker, Aboriginal Poet," *Denver Quarterly* 15, no. 4 (1991): 63–75, and "Twin Karma," Mason's introduction to Mark Twain's *The American Claimant* (New York: Oxford University Press, 1996), xxxi–xliii.

3. Michal Smith, "Bobbie Ann Mason, Artist and Rebel," *Kentucky Review* 8, no. 3 (Fall 1988): 60.

4. Bobbie Ann Mason, *The Girl Sleuth: A Feminist Guide to the Bobbsey Twins, Nancy Drew and Their Sisters* (New York: Feminist Press, 1975), 4.

5. Mason, *The Girl Sleuth,* 120.

6. See Lila Havens, "Residents and Transients: An Interview with Bobbie Ann Mason." *Crazyhorse* 29 (Fall 1985): 103; Michal Smith, "Bobbie Ann Mason," 60; Dorothy Combs Hill, "An Interview with Bobbie Ann Mason," *Southern Quarterly* 31, no. 1 (Fall 1992): 110, and Mason's account of this in "Reaching the Stars: My Life As a Fifties Groupie," *New Yorker,* 26 May 1986, 55.

7. Mason, "Reaching the Stars," 30–38.

8. Mason, "Reaching the Stars," 75.

9. Mason, *The Girl Sleuth,* ix.

10. Mervyn Rothstein, "Homegrown Fiction: Bobbie Ann Mason

Blends Springsteen and Nabokov," interview with Mason, *New York Times Magazine,* 15 May 1988, 99.

11. For "dirty realism," see Bill Buford's editorial in *Dirty Realism: New Writing From America, Granta* 8 (1983), 4–5. For "K-Mart Realism" and "minimalism," see John Barth's "A Few Words About Minimalism," *New York Times Book Review,* 28 Dec 1986, 1, 2, 25. Mason humorously alludes to Barth's coinage of the label "blue-collar minimalist hyper-realist" in her interview with Havens, "Residents and Transients," 95.

12. Havens, "Residents and Transients," 90.

13. The second collection of dirty realist writing was published as *More Dirt: New Writing from America,* ed. Bill Buford, *Granta* 19 (Summer 1986).

14. Buford, *Dirty Realism,* 4–5.

15. Buford, *Dirty Realism,* 5.

16. See Barth, "A Few Words About Minimalism;" Robert Dunn, "Fiction That Shrinks From Life," *New York Times Book Review,* 30 June 1985, 13, 24, 25; and Ben Yagoda, "No Tense Like the Present," *New York Times Book Review,* 10 Aug 1986, 6, 30.

17. Barbara Henning, "Minimalism and the American Dream: 'Shiloh' by Bobbie Ann Mason and 'Preservation' by Raymond Carver," *Modern Fiction Studies* 35, no. 4 (Winter 1989): 690.

18. See Combs Hill, "An Interview with Bobbie Ann Mason," 105, and Albert E. Wilhelm, "An Interview with Bobbie Ann Mason," *Southern Quarterly* 26, no. 2 (Winter 1988): 31.

19.Bobbie Ann Mason, *Nabokov's Garden: A Guide to Ada* (Ann Arbor, Michigan: Ardis, 1974), 139–41.

20. For Mason discussing the writing process, see Havens, "Residents and Transients," 96–99, and Lyons and Oliver, "An Interview with Bobbie Ann Mason," *Contemporary Literature* 32, no. 4 (Winter 1991): 450–51.

21. For Mason's comments on her "anti-elitism," see Michal Smith, "Bobbie Ann Mason," 61, and Combs Hill, "An Interview with Bobbie Ann Mason," 111.

22. Mason, *The Girl Sleuth,* x.

23. Mason, *Nabokov's Garden,* 69.

24. Mason, *The Girl Sleuth,* ix.

25. Craig Gholson, "Bobbie Ann Mason," *Bomb* 28 (Summer 1989): 42.

26. Gholson, "Bobbie Ann Mason," 40.

27. Mason, "The Way We Lived: The Chicken Tower," *New Yorker,* 16 October 1995, 92.

28. Combs Hill, "An Interview with Bobbie Ann Mason," 105.

29. Gholson, "Bobbie Ann Mason," 42.

30. Havens, "Residents and Transients," 95.

31. Havens, "Residents and Transients," 93.

32. Lyons and Oliver, "An Interview with Bobbie Ann Mason," 453.

33. See Mason, "Twin Karma," and "Huck, Continued," *New Yorker,* 26 June 1995, 130, a précis of the ideas which were to appear in "Twin Karma."

34. Mason, "Twin Karma," xli.

35. Mason, "Twin Karma," xxxii, xxxiii.

36. Havens, "Residents and Transients," 95.

37. "Bobbie Ann Mason," in *World Authors,* 1980–1985, ed. Vineta Colby (New York: H. W. Wilson, 1991), 590. Mason elaborates on this point in Lyons and Oliver, "An Interview with Bobbie Ann Mason," 454–55, and Havens, "Residents and Transients," 95.

38. Combs Hill, "An Interview with Bobbie Ann Mason," 90–91.

39. The conflict between what is promised by class mobility in the states and what it delivers is perceptively analyzed by Richard Sennett and Jonathan Cobb in *The Hidden Injuries of Class* (Cam-

bridge, England: Cambridge University Press, 1972). In particular, they note that the American class system "wounds" its originally working-class subjects by perpetuating in them "a hidden weight, a hidden anxiety, in the *quality* of experience, a matter of feeling inadequately in control" (33–34).

40. Duncan Webster, *Looka Yonder! The Imaginary America of Populist Culture* (London and New York: Routledge, 1988), 4.

41. See Moritz et al., eds., *Current Biography,* 32, and Gholson, "Bobbie Ann Mason," 42.

42. The variations on this theme are discussed by Combs Hill in "An Interview with Bobbie Ann Mason," 87; Havens in "Residents and Transients," 88; and Wendy Smith in "*Publishers Weekly* Interviews Bobbie Ann Mason," *Publishers Weekly* 228 (30 August 1985): 425.

43. See Webster's discussion of "agribusiness" in *Looka Yonder!,* 37, and David R. Pichaske's introduction to *Late Harvest, Rural American Writing,* ed. Pichaske (New York: Paragon House, 1991), 4–6.

44. Fred Hobson, in *The Southern Writer in the Postmodern World* (Athens: University of Georgia Press, 1991), locates Mason's work in a tradition of Southern writing as he finds there a continued preoccupation with the themes of "closeness to nature . . . attention to and affection for place, a close attention to family" (3) and attention to community, although he observes that in the society depicted by Mason, these concepts are being inexorably altered.

45. Havens, "Residents and Transients," 94.

46. See G.O. Morphew's discussion of this in "Downhome Feminists in *Shiloh and Other Stories,*" *Southern Literary Journal* 21, no. 2 (Spring 1989): 41–49.

47. Havens, "Residents and Transients," 94.

48. For an analysis of the role of ritual in Mason's work, see Dar-

lene Reimers Hill, "'Use To, the Menfolks Would Eat First': Food and Food Rituals in the Fiction of Bobbie Ann Mason," *Southern Quarterly* 30, no. 2–3 (Winter–Spring 1992): 81–89, and Albert E. Wilhelm, "Private Rituals: Coping with Change in the Fiction of Bobbie Ann Mason," *Midwest Quarterly* 29, no. 2 (Winter 1987): 271–82.

49. For an interpretation of the function of popular culture in the lives of Mason's characters, see Robert H. Brinkmeyer, "Never Stop Rocking: Bobbie Ann Mason and Rock-and-Roll," *Mississippi Quarterly* 42, no. 1 (Winter 1988–89): 5–17, and Leslie White, "The Function of Popular Culture in Bobbie Ann Mason's *Shiloh and Other Stories* and *In Country*," *Southern Quarterly* 25, no. 4 (Summer 1988): 69–79.

50. Fredric Jameson, "Postmodernism and Consumer Society," in *Postmodern Culture,* ed. Hal Foster (London: Pluto, 1985), 125. An expanded version of this essay appears as "The Cultural Logic of Late Capitalism" in his *Postmodernism; or, The Cultural Logic of Late Capitalism,* (London and New York: Verso, 1991), 1–54. A similar argument is put forward by Cecelia Tichi in "Video Novels," *Boston Review* 13, no. 3 (June 1987): 13. Tichi contends that many contemporary works of fiction about "television culture" emulate the experience of time created by television, projecting "a reality that is ongoing and in-the-moment, the moment itself endlessly protracted."

51. Jameson, "Postmodernism and Consumer Society," 125.

52. Jameson, *Postmodernism; or, The Cultural Logic of Late Capitalism,* 373.

53. Yagoda, "No Tense Like the Present," 30. John Barth also speculates that one of the factors which has produced contemporary minimalist writing is "an ever-dwindling readerly attention span," in "A Few Words About Minimalism," 25.

54. Robert Dunn, "Fiction That Shrinks From Life," 24.

55. Yagoda, "No Tense Like the Present," 30.

56. Dunn, citing T. S. Eliot, in "Fiction That Shrinks from Life," 24.

57. Andrew Levy, *The Culture and Commerce of the American Short Story* (Cambridge, England, and New York: Cambridge University Press, 1993), 2.

58. Levy, *The Culture and Commerce of the American Short Story,* 13.

59. Levy, *The Culture and Commerce of the American Short Story,* 2, quoting Peter Prescott's introduction to the *Norton Book of American Short Stories* (New York: W. W. Norton, 1988), 14.

60. For example, Fred Hobson comments in *The Southern Writer in the Postmodern World,* 19, that "one wonders, finally, if *In Country* . . . immerses itself too completely and uncritically in throw-away culture, and in the process—by showing us the world through the eyes of a character who focuses altogether on television and rock music and shopping malls—runs the risk of itself becoming a product of the throwaway culture it depicts, as lasting as and no more lasting than (that is, as dispensable as) M*A*S*H and rock music circa 1984."

61. The departure of many contemporary Southern writers from the concerns of their forbears, including both the Civil War and its legacy, and the civil rights era, is discussed by Fred Hobson in the opening chapter of *The Southern Writer in the Postmodern World,* 1–10. Mason herself has observed in "Across the Divide," her contribution to *Picturing the South, 1860 to the Present,* edited by Ellen Duggan (San Francisco: Chronicle, 1996), that growing up in Western Kentucky, where "only a small percentage of the overall population were black," she had "little opportunity to learn about a culture that existed right in my town" (140). Her main access to "the taboo black culture" was through listening to rhythm-and-blues music on the radio on WLAC, Nashville. In her commentary on her selection of photographs for inclusion in the exhibition "Picturing the South" (which was on view at the High Museum of Art, Folk Art and Photography

Galleries, Atlanta, Georgia, from 15 June to 14 September 1996), Mason observes that the photographs highlight the effects of segregation, which blighted the South during her childhood, showing both black and white people "trapped in isolation" (142).

Chapter Two: *Shiloh and Other Stories*

1. Robert Towers, "American Graffiti," *New York Times Book Review,* 16 December 1982, 39.

2. Anne Tyler, "Kentucky Cameos," *New Republic* 187, no. 1 (1 November 1982): 38.

3. Tyler, "Kentucky Cameos," 38.

4. Mason, "A Conversation with Bobbie Ann Mason," ed. David Y. Todd, *Boulevard* 4–5.3–1 (Spring 1990): 135, quoted by Andrew Levy in *The Culture and Commerce of the American Short Story,* 112.

5. Havens, "Residents and Transients," 88.

6. Levy, *The Culture and Commerce of the American Short Story,* 112.

7. Levy, *The Culture and Commerce of the American Short Story,* 113.

8. Dunn, "Fiction that Shrinks From Life," 13, 24, 25.

9. Barth, "A Few Words about Minimalism," and Yagoda, "No Tense like the Present."

10. Yagoda, "No Tense like the Present," 30.

11. Bobbie Ann Mason, *Shiloh and Other Stories* (New York: Harper and Row, 1982), 121. All parenthetical citations for *Shiloh and Other Stories* are from this edition.

12. Terry Thompson, "Mason's 'Shiloh,'" *Explicator* 54, no. 1 (Fall 1995): 55.

13. Mason, *Nabokov's Garden,* 143.

14. See Henning's reading of this passage in "Minimalism and the American Dream," 691.

15. Bobbie Ann Mason, *Midnight Magic* (Hopewell, N.J.: Ecco Press, 1998), xi.

16. See Reimers Hill's discussion of the connection between food, ritual, and gender in this story in "'Use To, the Menfolks Would Eat First,'" 85–87.

17. Albert Wilhelm, *Bobbie Ann Mason: A Study of the Short Fiction* (New York: Twayne–Prentice Hall, 1998), 50. Wilhelm is referring to Tina Bucher, "Changing Roles and Finding Stability: Women in Bobbie Ann Mason's *Shiloh and Other Stories," Border States: Journal of the Kentucky–Tennessee American Studies Association* 8 (1991): 54.

18. Wilhelm, *Bobbie Ann Mason,* 50.

19. See Reimers Hill's interpretation of this scene in "'Use to, the Menfolks Would Eat First,'" 85.

20. Linda Adams Barnes, "The Freak Endures: The Southern Grotesque from Flannery O'Connor to Bobbie Ann Mason," in *Since Flannery O'Connor: Essays On The Contemporary American Short Story,* ed. Loren Logsden and Charles W. Mayer (Macomb: Western Illinois University Press, 1987), 133–41.

21. Webster, *Looka Yonder!,* 116.

22. Mason has described how she writes by starting with a surface detail or line of dialogue to trigger getting inside a character or situation in Havens, "Residents and Transients," 97.

23. Mason has remarked of Nabokov that "his extraordinary childhood allowed him to indulge a child's way of seeing that's up close and particular"; interview with Lyons and Oliver, 461. In her article "The Elements of E. B. White's Style," *Language Arts* 56, no. 6 (Sept. 1979): 693, Mason also expressed her admiration of E. B. White's *Charlotte's Web,* in which White "asks adults to renew their

sense of wonder, and he asks children to try to understand the nature of reality."

24. See Barnes, "The Freak Endures," 140.

25. See Robert H. Brinkmeyer Jr.'s discussion of this story in "Finding One's History: Bobbie Ann Mason and Contemporary Southern Literature," *Southern Literary Journal* 19, no. 2 (Spring 1987): 26–27.

Chapter Three: *In Country*

1. For a discussion of Norman Jewison's adaptation of *In Country,* see Barbara Tepa Lupack, "History as Her-Story: Adapting Bobbie Ann Mason's *In Country* to Film," in *Vision/Re-Vision: Adapting Contemporary American Fiction by Women to Film,* ed. Tepa Lupack (Bowling Green: Bowling Green State University Popular Press, 1996), 159–92.

2. Joel Conarroe, "Winning Her Father's War," *New York Times Book Review* 15 (September 1985): 7.

3. Mason, "A Conversation with Bobbie Ann Mason," ed. David Y. Todd, *Boulevard* 4–5.3–1 (Spring 1990): 134, quoted by Levy, *The Culture and Commerce of the American Short Story,* 120.

4. Wilhelm, "An Interview with Bobbie Ann Mason," 29.

5. Mason, *The Girl Sleuth,* 6.

6. Mason, *The Girl Sleuth,* 13.

7. Mason, *The Girl Sleuth*, 74.

8. Mason, *The Girl Sleuth,* 75.

9. David Booth, "Sam's Quest, Emmett's Wound: Grail Motifs in Bobbie Ann Mason's Portrait of America After Vietnam," *Southern Literary Journal* 23, no. 2 (Spring 1991): 102.

10. Hobson, *The Southern Writer in the Postmodern World,* 18.

11. Hobson, *The Southern Writer the Postmodern World,* 19.

12. Conarroe, "Winning Her Father's War," 7.

13. For discussions of Sam's role as a reader of cultural "texts," see: June Dwyer, "New Roles, New History and New Patriotism: Bobbie Ann Mason's *In Country*," *Modern Language Studies* 22, no. 2 (Spring 1992): 72–78; Yonka Krasteva, "The South and The West in Bobbie Ann Mason's *In Country*," *Southern Literary Journal* 26, no. 2 (Spring 1994): 77–90; and Barbara T. Ryan, "Decentered Authority in Bobbie Ann Mason's *In Country*," *Critique: Studies in Contemporary Fiction* 31, no. 3 (Spring 1990): 199–212.

14. Wilhelm, *Bobbie Ann Mason*, 6.

15. Krasteva, "The South and the West," 81.

16. Krasteva, "The South and The West," 77.

17. Bobbie Ann Mason, *In Country* (New York: Harper and Row, 1985), 23. Further references will be given in the text.

18. See Katherine Kinney, "'Humping the Boonies': Sex, Combat and the Female in Bobbie Ann Mason's *In Country*," in *Fourteen Landing Zones: Approaches to Vietnam War Literature*, ed. Philip K. Jason (Iowa City: University of Iowa Press, 1991), 44–45.

19. Mason, *The Girl Sleuth*, 46.

20. Mason, *The Girl Sleuth*, 55.

21. The significance of food, and changing patterns of consumption, recur as indices of social change in Mason's work. In "The Burden of the Feast," *New Yorker*, 22 December 1997, 66, Mason recalls, "When I was growing up on our fifty-three-acre dairy farm, we were obsessed with food. Food was the center of our lives. Everything we did, every day, revolved around it. We planted it, grew it, harvested it, peeled it, cooked it, served it, consumed it—endlessly, day after day, season after season." She continues: "Life for our family was haunted by the fear of crop failure. We ate as if we didn't know where our next meal might come from. All my life, I have had a recurrent food dream: I face a buffet or cafeteria line, laden with beautiful foods. I spend the entire

dream choosing the foods I want. The anticipation of eating them is deliciously agonizing. I always wake up just as I've made my selections but before I get to eat." Michal Smith, in "Bobbie Ann Mason," 57, has interpreted Mason's reference to the "recurrent food dream" as suggesting that "today, food is perhaps the best example of the myriad of choices and the dilemma they pose in contemporary life." Mason herself has linked literal with ideological consumption in America, commenting in Combs Hill, "An Interview with Bobbie Ann Mason," 114, on her "goal-oriented" "training" in school "to be a consumer of knowledge and experience. . . . So I have this appetite to consume experience and—but on the literal level I like food," and, in *The Girl Sleuth*, 45–46: "If the goal is the big time, then there is no earthly way to get there except through the process of consuming. The American dream is the desire to absorb, know and conquer everything, to go everywhere and do it all, and to take whatever is free, even if you can't use it."

22. Michael Herr, *Dispatches* (London: Picador, 1979), 11.

23. Neil Campbell and Alasdair Kean, *American Cultural Studies: An Introduction to American Culture* (London and New York: Routledge, 1997), 278.

24. See Matthew C. Stewart, "Realism, Verisimilitude and the Depiction of Vietnam Veterans in *In Country*," in *Fourteen Landing Zones*, ed. Jason, 167, and Thomas Myers, "Dispatches from Ghost Country: the Vietnam Veteran in Recent American Fiction," *Genre* 21, no. 4 (Winter 1988): 424.

25. Myers, "Dispatches from Ghost Country," 412–13.

26. Myers, "Dispatches from Ghost Country," 422.

27. Bobbie Ann Mason, statement in "Generation of Fellows: Grants to Individuals from the National Endowment for the Arts," ed. Philip Kopper (National Endowment for the Arts, October 1983).

28. An example of this process is the work of the New York Vietnam Veterans Memorial Commission established by Edward I. Koch,

the mayor of New York, in the fall of 1982. Koch has described the commission as "an extraordinary example of how a community can begin to heal the wounds inflicted by the Vietnam War and to pay back the debt it owes to those who have suffered and sacrificed in its service," in his preface to *Dear America: Letters Home From Vietnam,* ed. Bernard Edelman (New York: Pocket Books–Simon & Schuster, 1985), 16. Koch recounts how "the commission sponsored a design competition" which produced the monument that was built in the Vietnam Veterans Plaza in New York and dedicated on 7 May 1985. The Commission also published requests for testimonial material from veterans, in response to which "some 3,000 letters, tapes, poems, newspaper clippings, petitions, journal entries . . . were submitted by 600 individuals," excerpts from some of which are etched onto the memorial to Vietnam veterans in New York (23). A selection of the letters is published in *Dear America.*

29. In "Dispatches from Ghost Country," 414, Myers observes that amongst veterans, even those who have outwardly adjusted to society, "there is the apprehension of difference . . . a shared, often unspoken knowledge that an unprecedented event *has* transformed the culture, and transformed most deeply and permanently those who were its most telling instruments."

30. Herr, *Dispatches,* 42.

31. For a discussion of the allusions to Springsteen in *In Country,* see Brinkmeyer, "Never Stop Rocking," 6.

32. In *The Remasculinization of America: Gender and the Vietnam War* (Bloomington and Indianapolis: Indiana University Press, 1989), Susan Jeffords argues that images of and narratives about masculinity in popular cultural representations of the Vietnam war are being used to "remasculinize" American culture. This remasculinization, Jeffords proposes, is a response to the anxiety caused by the loss of fathers, brothers, and sons in the war; the perceived emasculation of

the American government and its bureaucracy through the outcome of the war; and the challenge made to patriarchy made by such oppositional movements as the civil rights and women's rights movements.

33. See Ellen A. Blais's discussion of this in "Gender Issues in Bobbie Ann Mason's *In Country,*" *South Atlantic Review* 56, no. 2 (May 1991): 112.

34. See Ryan, "Decentered Authority," 199–203.

35. Kinney, "'Humping the Boonies': Sex, Combat and the Female," 45.

36. See Linden Peach's discussion of this episode in "'K Marts and Lost Parents': 'Dirty Realism' in Contemporary American and Irish Fiction," *Critical Survey* 9, no. 2 (1997): 65.

37. See Duncan Webster's discussion of the "struggles . . . over the meanings of tradition" which are articulated by Springsteen's music through his attempts "to create a patriotism against conservatism, linking pride in his country with extensive criticism of its policies," *Looka Yonder!,* 5.

38. Lin's first comment is from *U.S. News and World Report,* 21 November 1983, 68. Her second remark was made in *American Institute of Architects Journal* 72 (May 1983): 151. Both are quoted by Charles L. Griswold in "The Vietnam Veterans Memorial and the Washington Mall: Philosophical Thoughts on Political Iconography," *Critical Inquiry* 12 (Summer 1986): 716.

39. See Griswold, "The Vietnam Veterans Memorial," 692.

40. Campbell and Kean, *American Cultural Studies,* 260.

41. Albert Wilhelm has noted, in "Bobbie Ann Mason: Searching for Home," *Southern Writers at Century's End,* (Lexington: University Press of Kentucky, 1997), 162, that "Mason . . . had a similar experience at the wall that influenced her writing of *In Country.* In describing a visit to the memorial in 1983, she says: 'Quite by accident, my eyes fell upon my own name on the wall, a version of my

name—Bobby G. Mason. I found out later that Bobby G. Mason was from Florida. I learned also that there were four guys named Robert Mason whose names were on the wall. . . . I knew then that Vietnam was my story too, and it was every American's story. Finally, I felt I had a right to tell a small part of that story.'"

42. Diane Johnson, "Southern Comfort," *New York Times Book Review,* 7 November 1985, 16, cited by Myers in "Dispatches from Ghost Country," 424.

43. Krasteva, "The South and the West," 80.

44. Stewart, "Realism, Verisimilitude and the Depiction of Vietnam Veterans," 177.

45. James Campbell, "Coming Home: Difference and Reconciliation in Narratives of Return to "the World,'" in *The United States and Viet Nam: From War to Peace,* ed. Richard M. Slabey, (Jefferson, N.C.: McFarland, 1996), 200.

46. Campbell, "Coming Home," 200.

47. Campbell, "Coming Home," 203.

48. Jeffords, *The Remasculinization of America,* 62–65.

49. See Krasteva, "The South and The West," 88.

Chapter Four: *Spence + Lila* and *Love Life*

1. Bobbie Ann Mason, "The Way We Lived: The Chicken Tower," *New Yorker,* 10 February 1998, 86–88.

2. See Wilhelm's discussion of this, Bobbie Ann Mason, 9.

3. Mason, "The Way We Lived," 88.

4. Mason, "The Way We Lived," 90.

5. Mason, "Letter From Kentucky: Doing the Boptrot," *New Yorker,* 9 May 1994, 46.

6. Mason, "The Way We Lived," 96.

7. Mason, "Doing the Boptrot," 46.

8. Mason, "The Way We Lived," 88.

9. On the Kentucky Network program, "Bobbie Ann Mason," 1995, dir. Marsha Cooper Hellard, Hellard observed to Mason that *Spence + Lila* "grew out a family crisis." Mason explained: "My mother had been in hospital and had had a life-threatening illness, and so that is an experience that you have to deal with some way, and of course, my way is always writing."

10. Bobbie Ann Mason, *Spence + Lila* (London: Chatto & Windus, 1989), 13. Further references will be given in the text.

11. In *The Lost Continent: Travels in Small Town America* (London: Abacus–Little Brown, 1993) Bill Bryson refers to the Burma Shave signs as being representative of the passing of a distinctive Kentucky culture, as he reflects on the "sad loss" of the identity of individual states due to the homogenization of contemporary "American" culture. His description, when compared with Mason's, also underlines the realism which Mason achieves, using precisely observed detail to make sharp social commentary. Bryson writes: "I drove through Kentucky thinking of sad losses and was abruptly struck by the saddest loss of all—the Burma Shave sign. Burma Shave was a shaving cream that came in a tube. I don't know if it's still produced. In fact, I never knew anyone who ever used it. But the Burma Shave company used to put clever signs along the highway. They came in clusters of five, so that you read a little poem as you passed: IF HARMONY/IS WHAT YOU CRAVE/THEN GET/A TUBA/BURMA SHAVE. . . . Even in the 1950s, the Burma Shave signs were pretty much a thing of the past. I can only remember seeing half a dozen in all the thousands of highways we covered" (53–54).

12. Devon Jersild, "The World of Bobbie Ann Mason," *Kenyon Review* 11 (1989): 165.

13. Mason, "The Way We Lived," 96.

14. Jersild, "The World of Bobbie Ann Mason," 167.

15. Lorrie Moore, "What Li'l Abner Said," *New York Times Book Review,* 12 March 1989, 7.

16. Moore, "What Li'l Abner Said," 7.

17. Jersild, "The World of Bobbie Ann Mason," 165.

18. Jersild, "The World of Bobbie Ann Mason," 169.

19. Moore, "What Li'l Abner Said," 9.

20. Bobbie Ann Mason, *Love Life* (London: Chatto & Windus, 1989), 1. Further references will be given in the text.

21. Wilhelm, *Bobbie Ann Mason,* 95.

22. Albert Wilhelm notes that "Mason wrote this story while she was working on . . . *In Country,*" in *Bobbie Ann Mason,* 83.

23. Mason returns to this subject in "Recycling Kentucky," *New Yorker,* 1 November 1993, 50–62, where she reviews Robert Schenkkan's play, "The Kentucky Cycle," about "the interwoven histories of three families from the time Eastern Kentucky is settled, through the Civil War, and up to the present era of strip-mining" (50). While being sensitive to Schenkkan's professed intention to portray the devastation of the landscape by the mining of the coal seams, the poverty endured by the strip-mine workers, and their exploitation by the wealthy mine owners, Mason also entertains criticisms of the play which maintain that it stereotypes the people of Appalachia as hillbillies, in order that they can bear the "shame and guilt" of the failure of the American Dream through "violence and greed" (60).

24. Mason, *Midnight Magic: Selected Stories of Bobbie Ann Mason* (Hopewell, N.J.: Ecco Press, 1998), x, xi.

25. Wilhelm, *Bobbie Ann Mason,* 125.

26. Wilhelm, *Bobbie Ann Mason,* 11.

Chapter Five: *Feather Crowns*

1. Wilhelm, *Bobbie Ann Mason,* 130.

2. Kentucky Network, "Bobbie Ann Mason."

3. Mason, "The Way We Lived," 90.

4. Bobbie Ann Mason, "The Mystery of My Grandmother's Mind," in *Southern Women,* ed. Marc Smirnoff, special issue of *Oxford American* 26 (March–May 1999): 23.

5. Mason, "The Mystery of My Grandmother's Mind," 24.

6. Mason, "The Mystery of My Grandmother's Mind," 22.

7. Mason, "The Way We Lived," 88.

8. Kentucky Network, "Bobbie Ann Mason."

9. Michael Kreyling used this term to describe *Feather Crowns* in Kentucky Network's "Bobbie Ann Mason."

10. See Harriet Pollack's discussion of how Mason "recenters history," in "From *Shiloh* to *In Country* to *Feather Crowns*: Bobbie Ann Mason, Women's History, and Southern Fiction," *Southern Literary Journal* 28: 2 (Spring 1996): 95–96.

11. Pollack, "From *Shiloh* to *In Country* to *Feather Crowns,*" 102.

12. Pollack, "From *Shiloh* to *In Country* to *Feather Crowns,*" 114.

13. In Kentucky Network's "Bobbie Ann Mason," Mason has explained that "One reason I seized on this [Christianna Wheeler's] story is that I felt that it gave me an avenue, a way of writing about my grandparents' world, the world they grew up in, and to me, writing about the past and writing about that part of the world was very natural and really a part of what I write about in a contemporary sense, because it filled out for me where my characters come from, and why they are the way they are."

14. Pollack, "From *Shiloh* to *In Country* to *Feather Crowns,*" 103.

15. Guy Debord, *Society of the Spectacle,* trans. Donald Nicholson-Smith (New York: Zone, 1994), 29, para. 42.

16. Debord, *Society of the Spectacle,* 12, para 4.

17. Julia Kristeva, "Women's Time," trans. Alice Jardine and

Harry Blake, in *The Kristeva Reader,* ed. Toril Moi (Oxford, England: Basil Blackwell, 1986), 189. Kristeva argues that the symbols which a group, for example, a nation, hands down across the generations, allow the perpetuation of a common understanding and interpretation of these phenomena. This commonality, borne in collective memory, contributes to the constitution of a community, she proposes.

18. Kentucky Network, "Bobbie Ann Mason."

19. Jacqueline Rose, "The Cult of Celebrity," *New Formations* 36 (1999): 19.

20. Bobbie Ann Mason, *Feather Crowns* (London: Chatto & Windus, 1993), 3. Further references will be given in the text.

21. Pollack, "From *Shiloh* to *In Country* to *Feather Crowns,*" 104.

22. Bobbie Ann Mason, interview with Albert Wilhelm, in *Bobbie Ann Mason,* 130.

23. Pollack, "From *Shiloh* to *In Country* to *Feather Crowns,*" 108.

24. Pollack, "From *Shiloh* to *In Country* to *Feather Crowns,*" 111.

25. Rose, "The Cult of Celebrity," 16.

26. Rose, "The Cult of Celebrity," 10.

27. Rose, "The Cult of Celebrity," 12.

28. See Pollack's discussion of this in "From *Shiloh* to *In Country* to *Feather Crowns,*" 107.

29. Pollack, "From *Shiloh* to *In Country* to *Feather Crowns,*" 112.

30. Sarah Wood, "Home Values: Ann Romines, *The Home Plot* and Bobbie Ann Mason, *Feather Crowns,*" *Over Here* 14, no. 1 (Summer 1994): 97.

31. Sarah Wood, "Home Values," 97.

32. Pollack, "From *Shiloh* to In Country to *Feather Crowns,*" 109.

33. Pollack, "From *Shiloh* to *In Country* to *Feather Crowns*," 110.

34. Pollack, "From *Shiloh* to *In Country* to *Feather Crowns*," 110.

Books by Bobbie Ann Mason

Nabokov's Garden: A Guide to Ada. Ann Arbor, Michigan: Ardis, 1974.

The Girl Sleuth: A Feminist Guide to the Bobbsey Twins, Nancy Drew and Their Sisters. New York: Feminist Press, 1975. Reissued with new preface by Mason. Athens: University of Georgia Press, 1995.

Shiloh and Other Stories. New York: Harper and Row, 1982; Lexington, Kentucky: University Press of Kentucky, 1995; London: Chatto and Windus, 1983.

In Country. New York: Harper and Row, 1985; London: Chatto and Windus, 1986.

Spence + Lila. New York: Harper and Row, 1988; London: Chatto and Windus, 1989.

Love Life. New York: Harper and Row, 1989; London: Chatto and Windus, 1989.

Feather Crowns. New York: HarperCollins, 1993; London: Chatto and Windus, 1993.

Midnight Magic. Hopewell, N.J.: Ecco Press, 1998. Comprises stories from previous collections, with a new introduction by the author: "Midnight Magic," "Bumblebees," "The Retreat," "Love Life," "Big Bertha Stories," "Shiloh," "Offerings," "Drawing Names," "Coyotes," "Residents and Transients," "Sorghum," "Nancy Culpepper," "Graveyard Day," "A New-Wave Format," "Third Monday," "Wish," and "Memphis."

Selected Nonfiction by Bobbie Ann Mason

"Across the Divide." In *Picturing the South: 1860 to the Present,* ed. Ellen Duggan (San Francisco: Chronicle Books, 1996), 140–73.

"The Elements of E. B. White's Style." *Language Arts* 56, no. 6 (September 1979): 692–96.

"The Mystery of My Grandmother's Mind." In *Southern Women,* ed. Marc Smirnoff. Special issue of *Oxford American* 26 (March–May 1999): 21–24.

"Nancy Drew: The Once and Future Prom Queen." In *Feminism in Women's Detective Fiction,* ed. Glenwood Irons (Toronto: University of Toronto Press, 1995), 74–93.

"Reaching the Stars: My Life As A Fifties Groupie." *New Yorker,* 26 May 1986, 30–38. Reprinted in *A World Unsuspected: Portraits of a Southern Childhood,* ed. Alex Harris (Chapel Hill: University of North Carolina Press, 1987), 53–77.

"Twin Karma." Introduction to Mark Twain's *The American Claimant* (1892) (New York: Oxford University Press, 1996), xxxi–xliii.

"The Way We Lived: The Chicken Tower." *New Yorker,* 16 October 1995, 85–97.

Interviews, Personal Statements, and Biographical Sketches

Bobbie Ann Mason. Signature, Program 101. Dir. Marsha Cooper Hellard. Prod. Guy Mendes. Videotape ed. James Walker. Narr. Marsha Cooper Hellard. Kentucky Network, Lexington. 1995. Informative program in which Mason discusses her life and work.

Bonnetti, Kay. "Bobbie Ann Mason." Interview. Columbia, Mo.: American Audio Prose Library, 1985. Discusses the influences on Mason's "writing life" and her literary treatment of "people in transit from the old to the new South."

Gholson, Craig. "Bobbie Ann Mason." *Bomb* 28 (Summer 1989): 40–43. Interview. Mason discusses the role of the changing South

BIBLIOGRAPHY

and the connection of language to place and class in her work and defends the function of television in her characters' lives.

Havens, Lila. "Residents and Transients: An Interview With Bobbie Ann Mason." *Crazyhorse* 29 (Fall 1985): 87–104. Mason discusses subjects such as the importance of her relationship with her parents and Kentucky to her writing, the role of popular music in her life and writing, and her interest in the effects of class mobility.

Hill, Dorothy Combs. "An Interview with Bobbie Ann Mason." *Southern Quarterly* 31, no. 1 (Fall 1992): 85–118. Mason discusses cultural and personal change, language, and her preoccupation with food.

Lyons, Bonnie and Oliver, Bill. "An Interview With Bobbie Ann Mason." *Contemporary Literature* 32, no. 4 (Winter 1991): 449–470. Includes biographical information and a discussion of the themes of Mason's fiction.

Rothstein, Mervyn. "Homegrown Fiction: Bobbie Ann Mason Blends Springsteen and Nabokov." *New York Times Magazine,* 15 May 1988, 50, 98, 99, 101,108. Account of interview, relating Mason's themes to her life.

Smith, Michal. "Bobbie Ann Mason, Artist and Rebel." *Kentucky Review* 8, no. 3 (Fall 1988): 56–63. Account of Mason's views about childhood influences upon her challenge to literary traditions.

Smith, Wendy. "*Publishers Weekly* Interviews Bobbie Ann Mason." *Publishers Weekly* 228 (30 August 1985): 424–425. Mason comments on writing *In Country* and how she regards herself as a Southern writer.

Wilhelm, Albert E. "An Interview with Bobbie Ann Mason." *Southern Quarterly* 26, no. 2 (Winter 1988): 27–38. Considers the themes and structure of *In Country.*

Critical Essays

Shiloh and Other Stories

Arnold, Edwin T. "Falling Apart and Staying Together: Bobbie Ann Mason and Leon Driskell Explore the State of the Modern Family." *Appalachian Journal* 12, no. 2 (Winter 1985): 135–141. Argues that the main theme of *Shiloh* is the negative effect of the tension between change and tradition on "shifting" modern relationships.

Barnes, Linda Adams. "The Freak Endures: The Southern Grotesque from Flannery O'Connor to Bobbie Ann Mason." In *Since Flannery O'Connor: Essays On The Contemporary American Short Story,* ed. Loren Logsden and Charles W. Mayer (Macomb: Western Illinois University Press, 1987), 133–41. A lucid exposition of O'Connor's concept of the grotesque and how Mason adapts this to create a "mundane" grotesque that is apposite to the "cultural crisis" engendered by the changing identity of the South.

Blythe, Hal, and Charlie Sweet. "The Ambiguous Grail Quest in 'Shiloh.'" *Studies in Short Fiction* 32 (Spring 1995): 223–26. Argues that "Shiloh" is a reworking of the grail myth, which gives it a unity that transcends its minimalist detail.

Brinkmeyer, Robert H., Jr. "Finding One's History: Bobbie Ann Mason and Contemporary Southern Literature." *Southern Literary Journal* 19, no. 2 (Spring 1987): 21–33. Compares Mason's vision of the South with Allen Tate's, through analysis of their respective insistence on the necessity of confronting the past in order to understand the self and society in the present.

————. "Never Stop Rocking: Bobbie Ann Mason and Rock-and-Roll." *Mississippi Quarterly* 42, no. 1 (Winter 1988–89): 5–17. Discusses the importance in Mason's fiction of popular music as a means of cultural expression enabling the growth of the self.

Giannone, Richard. "Bobbie Ann Mason and the Recovery of Mystery." *Studies in Short Fiction* 27, no. 4 (Fall 1990): 553–66. Focuses on "Shiloh," "The Retreat," and "Third Monday" to argue that Mason's stories present the demystification of contemporary life, while also being attuned to the mysteries of the everyday.

Henning, Barbara. "Minimalism and the American Dream: 'Shiloh' by Bobbie Ann Mason and 'Preservation' by Raymond Carver." *Modern Fiction Studies* 35, no. 4 (Winter 1989): 689–98. Excellent article that demonstrates how Mason's writing encourages the reader to create metaphoric frames through which to render meaningful the everyday details in which her characters are trapped.

Hill, Darlene Reimers. "'Use To, the Menfolks Would Eat First': Food and Food Rituals in the Fiction of Bobbie Ann Mason." *Southern Quarterly* 30, no. 2–3 (Winter–Spring 1992): 81–89. Shows how Mason explores the tension between change and tradition through her representation of the significance of food and its associated rituals in Southern culture.

Levy, Andrew. "Back Home Again: Bobbie Ann Mason's 'Shiloh.'" In *The Culture and Commerce of the American Short Story,* by Andrew Levy (Cambridge, England and New York: Cambridge University Press, 1993), 108–25. Thought-provoking and informative chapter that explores the contradictions in Mason's avowed populism and identifies her preoccupation with the "class struggle" as the main concern of her stories. This, Levy argues, is articulated through the tension between being at home or away from home, which is central to both her stories and her authorial persona.

Morphew, G. O. "Downhome Feminists in *Shiloh and Other Stories.*" *Southern Literary Journal* 21, no. 2 (Spring 1989): 41–49. Argues that many of Mason's women characters are responding to change in rural Kentucky by acquiring a feminist consciousness, but that this is part of a larger process of cultural homogenization through which they will lose their distinct identity.

BIBLIOGRAPHY

Ryan, Maureen. "'Stopping Places': Bobbie Ann Mason's Short Stories." In *Women Writers of the Contemporary South,* ed. Peggy Whitman Prenshaw (Jackson: University Press of Mississippi, 1984), 283–94. Examines Mason's characters' struggle to adapt to change in a Kentucky which is "paradigmatic of the contemporary South and to an extent of modern America."

Towers, Robert. "American Graffiti." *New Review of Books* 29 (16 December 1982): 38–40. Favorable review which examines the relation between "vision and technique" in *Shiloh.*

White, Leslie. "The Function of Popular Culture in Bobbie Ann Mason's *Shiloh and Other Stories* and *In Country.*" *Southern Quarterly* 25, no. 4 (Summer 1988): 69–79. Perceptively analyzes how Mason's work explores the variously liberating and deadening effects of popular culture on her characters.

Wilhelm, Albert E. "Making Over or Making Off: The Problem of Identity in Bobbie Ann Mason's Short Fiction." *Southern Literary Journal* 18, no. 2 (Spring 1985): 76–82. Examines the thematic patterns of Mason's characters' search for identity.

———. "Private Rituals: Coping with Change in the Fiction of Bobbie Ann Mason." *Midwest Quarterly* 29, no. 2 (Winter 1987): 271–282. Argues that Mason's stories show how contemporary individuals must improvise rituals to mark the transitions in their lives, as common rituals which establish the relation of the individual to the group have largely been lost.

———. *Bobbie Ann Mason: A Study of the Short Fiction* (New York: Twayne–Prentice Hall, 1998). A reading of the collected short stories, organized around the theme of the characters' attempts to find meaning or order through traveling, staying at home and cultivating gardens, or craftsmanship and artistry. Includes a chronology of Mason's life, a 1995 interview with Mason by Wilhelm, and reprints of Lyons and Oliver, 1991; Giannone, 1990; and White, 1988.

BIBLIOGRAPHY

In Country

Blais, Ellen A. "Gender Issues in Bobbie Ann Mason's *In Country*." *South Atlantic Review* 56, no. 2 (May 1991): 107–18. Examines the connection between the novel's exploration of the cultural effects of the war in Vietnam and its "subtextual" preoccupation with issues of gender.

Booth, David. "Sam's Quest, Emmett's Wound: Grail Motifs in Bobbie Ann Mason's Portrait of America After Vietnam." *Southern Literary Journal* 23, no. 2 (Spring 1991): 98–109. Reads *In Country* as a reworking of the grail myth, through Mason's depiction of Samantha's quest for meaning in the "waste land" of post-Vietnam American popular culture.

Campbell, James. "Coming Home: Difference and Reconciliation in Narratives of Return to 'the World.'" In *The United States and Viet Nam: From War to Peace,* ed. Richard M. Slabey (Jefferson, N.C.: McFarland, 1996), 198–207. Explores "the terms of sexual difference through which narratives of return" from Vietnam to America "have been constructed," in particular the significance of sexual relations between veterans and civilians as a metaphor of the possibility of reconciliation between them.

Conarroe, Joel. "Winning Her Father's War." *New York Times Book Review,* 15 September 1985, 7. Favorable review of *In Country* that introduces some of the novel's thematic and stylistic concerns.

Durham, Sandra Bonilla. "Women and War: Bobbie Ann Mason's *In Country*." *Southern Literary Journal* 22, no. 2 (Spring 1990): 45–52. Analyzes the novel's exploration of changing gender roles through the main characters' quests in post-Vietnam America.

Dwyer, June. "New Roles, New History and New Patriotism: Bobbie Ann Mason's *In Country*." *Modern Language Studies* 22, no. 2 (Spring 1992): 72–78. Argues that the establishment of a nonpatriarchal model of the family is central to the narrative, as it explores Samantha Hughes's role as a "new historian" and a "new patriot."

Hobson, Fred. "A Question of Culture—and History: Bobbie Ann Mason, Lee Smith, and Barry Hannah." In his *The Southern Writer in the Postmodern World* (Athens and London: University of Georgia Press, 1991): 11–40. Part of an examination of contemporary Southern fiction's continuities with and departures from earlier Southern writing. A thoughtful consideration of the extent to which the novel's investigation of a particular historical moment is limited by Sam Hughes's immersion in popular culture.

Kinney, Katherine. "'Humping the Boonies': Sex, Combat, and the Female in Bobbie Ann Mason's *In Country*." In *Fourteen Landing Zones: Approaches to Vietnam War Literature,* ed. Philip K. Jason (Iowa City: University of Iowa Press, 1991), 38–48. Discusses the novel's examination of the construction of gender through its reworking of the connections between metaphors of sex and war.

Krasteva, Yonka. "The South and The West in Bobbie Ann Mason's *In Country.*" *Southern Literary Journal* 26, no. 2 (Spring 1994): 77–90. Substantial article which explores how in *In Country,* national myths, particularly those associated with the frontier, are contested by the quest of a feminine protagonist. Learning to decipher "history" and the texts of her culture, she redefines concepts of home, community, family, and self.

Lupack, Barbara Tepa. "History as Her-Story: Adapting Bobbie Ann Mason's *In Country* to Film." In *Vision/Revision: Adapting Contemporary American Fiction by Women to Film,* ed. Barbara Tepa Lupack (Bowling Green, Ky.: Bowling Green State University Popular Press, 1996), 159–92. Appreciative analysis of the novel and film, but criticizes Jewison's change of focus from Sam to Emmett.

Myers, Thomas. "Dispatches from Ghost Country: the Vietnam Veteran in Recent American Fiction." *Genre* 21: 4 (Winter 1988):

BIBLIOGRAPHY

409–28. Contextualizes *In Country* through an informative analysis of the relation of representations of the Vietnam veteran to larger cultural shifts. Contends that although Mason uses existing American myths to interpret the war, the novel resists "reductive historical consensus."

Peach, Linden. "'K Marts and Lost Parents': 'Dirty Realism' in Contemporary American and Irish Fiction." *Critical Survey* 9, no. 2 (1997): 61–79. Analyzes the relation between such concepts as family, community, and gender and notions of identity, knowledge, and reality in American and Irish "dirty realist" writing, with particular reference to *In Country*.

Price, Joanna. "Remembering Vietnam: Subjectivity and Mourning in American New Realist Writing." *Journal of American Studies* 27, no. 2 (1993): 173–86. An analysis of the way in which the representation of the condition of mourning for American losses sustained in the Vietnam war provides both a symbol of and a structure for identity in consumer culture, in *In Country* and Jayne Anne Phillips's *Machine Dreams*.

Ryan, Barbara T. "Decentered Authority in Bobbie Ann Mason's *In Country*." *Critique: Studies in Contemporary Fiction* 31, no. 3 (Spring 1990): 199–212. A Derridean reading of the novel, which argues that Samantha Hughes moves from being a "structuralist" to a "poststructuralist" reader of her culture as she relinquishes her desire to locate absolute authority and truth in the word of her father in favor of an acceptance of the "dialogic" relation between self and "other."

Stewart, Matthew C. "Realism, Verisimilitude and the Depiction of Vietnam Veterans in *In Country*." In *Fourteen Landing Zones: Approaches to Vietnam War Literature,* ed. Philip K. Jason (Iowa City: University of Iowa Press, 1991), 166–79. Informative discussion of the experience of returned Vietnam veterans, but con-

strained by its assessment of the novel according to the verisimilitude of its representation of the veterans.

Albert E. Wilhelm. "Bobbie Ann Mason: Searching for Home." In
Southern Writers at Century's End, ed. Jeffrey Folks (Lexington:
University Press of Kentucky, 1997), 151–63. Discusses Mason's
representation of the "cultural dislocation" experienced by returning Vietnam veterans in "Big Bertha Stories" and *In Country.*

Spence + Lila and *Love Life*

Jersild, Devon. "The World of Bobbie Ann Mason." *Kenyon Review*
11 (1989): 163–69. Useful review which considers Mason's development of the themes of her earlier work in *Spence + Lila* and *Love
Life.*

Moore, Lorrie. "What Li'l Abner Said." *New York Times Book
Review,* 12 March 1989, 7, 9. Review article, offering insights into
Mason's use of the short-story form and her themes.

Feather Crowns

Pollack, Harriet. "From *Shiloh* to *In Country* to *Feather Crowns:* Bobbie Ann Mason, Women's History, and Southern Fiction." *Southern Literary Journal* 28, no. 2 (Spring 1996): 95–116. Analyzes
Mason's exploration of the "unofficial" histories of those marginalized by race, class, and gender, focusing on *Feather Crowns.*

Wood, Sarah. "Home Values: Ann Romines, *The Home Plot,* and
Bobbie Ann Mason, *Feather Crowns,*" *Over Here* 14, no. 1 (Summer 1994): 91–97. Review which draws attention to the relevance
of Mason's depiction of a turn-of-the-century community in transition to contemporary ethical debates about the relation between
the individual, family, and state.

BIBLIOGRAPHY

General

Barth, John. "A Few Words about Minimalism." *New York Times Book Review,* 28 December 1986, 1,2, 25. Witty commentary on the aesthetics of the "New American Short Story" and related social trends.

Dunn, Robert. "Fiction That Shrinks from Life." *New York Times Book Review,* 30 June 1985, 13, 24, 25. Argues that the diminished scope of "private interest" fiction is a result of the contemporary lack of a sense of the possibility of engaging with historical and cultural forces.

Newman, Charles. "What's Left Out of Literature." *New York Times Book Review,* 12 July 1987, 1, 24, 25. Proposes that contemporary minimalist fiction is "the chronicle of a climactic shattering of cultural bonds and social retrogression."

Yagoda, Ben. "No Tense like the Present." *New York Times Book Review,* 10 August 1986, 6, 30. Explores the reasons for and effect of the use of the present tense in fiction by contemporary "super-realists."

INDEX